Wm. Copenthwaite

A HANDMADE LIFE

IN SEARCH OF SIMPLICITY — WM. COPERTHWAITE

Photographs by Peter Forbes

CHELSEA GREEN PUBLISHING COMPANY — WHITE RIVER JUNCTION, VERMONT

CONTENTS

FOREWORD

It was just past midnight when I slipped my canoe into the water at Duck Cove and headed due east, exactly as the instructions said, to the point of shore where he would meet me. A green light clung to each of my paddle strokes. The bay was stunningly calm, and so silent that I could hear a pair of raccoons breaking open mussels on the distant shore. Our two canoes met and neither of us spoke a word, sensing that it was better to let the night speak for us. The moonlight cast long shadows on the spruce-lined shores and the channel narrowed, bringing us eventually to the powerful tiderip through which we passed to enter Bill's home. That evening, the tide was going our way and I rode the current, pulled deeper into a place that would change my life.

The rushing tide empties into a calm and large expanse of shallow water called Mill Pond, the heartbeat of Bill's homestead. Pulled by Earth's relationship to the moon, the pond fills and empties again twice a day, living a dramatic life of tides: waves of green water, mudflats, mussel beds, eagle, osprey, and heron. I've been coming here for ten years now and it's this ever-changing pond, the ebb and flow of seawater, that tells me I've arrived.

Bill and these four miles of coastline have gently shaped one another in a relationship that has lasted forty years, in which an enduring quality of care and attention has made him and the wilds inseparable. They live together. He's built osprey nests, gathered his water from hand-dug springs, and harvested mussels. He's made footpaths through the woods, where after years of pulling fir saplings by hand, he now walks through glades of birch and maple. He's transplanted the smallest of flowers and the heaviest of stones to make his place complete. He hammered rock to create a landing for his canoes, and he's built a beautiful home by hand from wood and sun.

Bill and I have crossed miles of open water to explore a stretch of beach that might yield rope, or whalebone, or a revealing conversation about abundance and fairness. Bill's life has quietly offered me the proof that an individual, in our country and in this age, can still create a unique and authentic life, and that the art of that life is in its wholeness with its place. In watching how Bill carries the land in his heart and mind, I have learned that the essential purpose of saving land is to create the chance that each of us, in our own way, might live in a healthy relationship with the rest of earthly life and—in so doing—to elevate what it means to be human. We need Bill's story to remind us of other ways of living.

I dedicate these images to my colleagues at Maine Coast Heritage Trust and the Trust for Public Land who are endeavoring to keep all life healthy at Dickinson's Reach, and to everyone who seeks a relationship with land in their own journey to lead a unique life.

Peter Forbes
Fayston, Vermont

THE CRAFT OF LIVING *by* JOHN SALTMARSH

The main thrust of my work is not simple living—not yurt design, not social change, although each of these is important and receives large blocks of my time. But they are not central. My central concern is encouragement—encouraging people to seek, to experiment, to plan, to create, and to dream. If enough people do this we will find a better way.

These are the words of Bill Coperthwaite. This book is about his lifelong commitment to living in a way that can create a world of justice, beauty, and hope.

Bill Coperthwaite has spent better than forty years on a homestead in the wilds of Maine. He has also traveled the globe in search of cultural skills, practices, and designs that can be blended and enhanced for contemporary use. He builds as much for joy in the process of building as for the beauty of the result. He is as devoted to working with his hands as he is to the highest ideals of democracy. He lives on the furthest margins of the market economy as an experiment in sustainable living.

Several themes anchor his life practices: education, nonviolence, simple living, democracy, and the fallacy of discipleship. Bill has developed his thinking in detail around each of these, yet they are interrelated and mutually reinforcing, and my attempt to give each area separate attention for the sake of clarity must oversimplify.

Bill's thoughts and actions have been profoundly shaped by those he describes as "people in particular whom I admired for their intellectual acuity, their work with their hands, and their dedication to a better society"—men such as Morris Mitchell, Richard Gregg, and Scott Nearing. Each of them influenced Bill in specific ways as he set his own course. He has neither followed nor looked to be followed, yet his way of being in the world embraces the linking of past, present, and future, providing a sense of irrefutable hope and abundant optimism.

EDUCATION

Bill's undergraduate years at Bowdoin College, in Brunswick, Maine, proved uninspiring. Real learning took place elsewhere, out of the classroom and away from campus. He read Gandhi on his own. He established connections with the International Student Center in Cambridge, Massachusetts, jumping a bus to spend weekends discovering a wider world than the one offered through "higher" education. A senior semester abroad at the University of Innsbruck stimulated a yearning for culture and perspective; he became an expatriate who reluctantly returned to Bowdoin to complete a degree in art history.

Through connections in Cambridge, he was invited to apply for graduate study by Morris Mitchell, the director of the Putney Graduate School of Teacher Education. Mitchell, renowned for his "slow moving, bold thinking" presence, had come to Putney with a reputation as a tenacious southern Quaker and visionary organizer of school-based rural cooperatives in Alabama and Georgia. His Quaker faith and experiences as a soldier in World War I had made him a resolute pacifist. As an educator, he embraced experiential education and the application of knowledge for social purposes. In Mitchell, Bill found a mentor who "blended cabinet-making and gardening with his leadership of the school." The students at Putney Graduate School were apprentices to a special view of education and the role of the teacher. "The life of a teacher," Mitchell instructed, "is as important a life as any person may live. Viewed broadly, it is a life of leadership in a world of contradictions and crisis. It is a particularly human life, one of total involvement with human beings as they face human questions."

Mitchell's students, and the future students they would teach, would need to possess certain kinds of knowledge, but he believed that knowledge alone was not sufficient; they would not be true teachers "unless they become also intelligent in the art of democratic living in a day of peace based on universally shared plenty." Mitchell was the first person who encouraged Bill to pursue his ideals and to put them into practice in his daily life.

Mitchell also modeled how a teacher may be both educator and learner. Not an authority of specialized knowledge, an expert who has all the answers and imparts some construction of "truth," the teacher is a designer of the learning process, a choreographer of discovery. Teachers value and respect the unique knowledge that others contribute to the learning experience and foster a mutually shared responsibility among all those involved in producing knowledge and learning. This ethos of education is the precursor to active participation in civic life and the training ground for an expansive practice of democracy. Neither education nor democracy is a passive experience, a spectator activity.

Traditional education, in Bill's view, puts children "behind a desk and make[s] them stay quiet and inactive for long periods of time from very early years, insisting that they learn material that is unrelated, for the most part, to their lives in any way they can see." To remedy this, he believes schools need to provide for "excitement and physical challenge through work and through living close to the natural forces of wind and sea."

Bill's educational ideal celebrates nonviolence and sets students free from dreary inactivity. What is often lacking in educational programs dedicated to nonviolence "is the need for excitement, physical challenge, danger, and the feeling of *camaraderie* or *esprit de corps* that these bring when experienced as a part of a group." In the past, Bill

explains, "war has provided this, as has the imminence of natural disaster in the form of storms, floods, etc., and to some degree sports such as football, boxing, or mountain climbing. Those who are searching for a nonviolent life tend to move toward the elimination of all these (with the exception of sports that do not involve bodily contact) and put little in their place." If it is to capture the imagination and attention of youth, education has to be "more challenging, exciting, and meaningful," expressing elation in the activities of everyday life and a learning process relevant to that life.

This is the philosophy behind the school that Bill envisioned creating in Maine. In a letter published in the magazine *Manas* in 1963, he outlined his guiding educational principles in this way:

— The school will adhere to Gandhi's admonition that the more money involved, the less development there will be.
— Education is the right of every child in the world, so schooling should be free to all who want to learn and are willing to work for the opportunity.
— The instructors at the school will work with their hands and back as well as with their heart and brain to build the school and work for social change through the betterment of education, serving without financial gain.
— Education will be more challenging, enjoyable, and exciting while providing more opportunity for contemplation and solitude.
— Aesthetics are central to the curriculum, since beauty is a birthright and the lack of beauty is a sign of great danger.
— Feeling useful and needed is essential to sound emotional growth.

- There is joy in hard physical labor.
- A close personal relationship with the natural world is of primary importance in the development of the individual.
- Every person has creative potential that should be nourished and helped to flower.
- Students should be invited to learn and not compelled, as learning at its best stems from the request of the student and not the demand of an authority.
- The development of skill with hands is of primary importance to full emotional and intellectual growth.

W. Coperthwaite

At one time Bill dreamed of creating this school on his own homestead on the coast of Maine. In some ways he has, although what now exists as the Yurt Foundation lacks conventional academic structures and organization. And there is no incoming or graduating class.

Build a yurt with Bill and you witness his educational ideas in action. The yurt is his philosophy made visible—security, nonviolence, simplicity, experimentation, activism, cultural blending, reverence for place, and beauty. He will not build a yurt for you (that would be tantamount to commodification of an educational experience), but he will work with you to build a yurt. As the structure takes shape, Bill emerges from the central hole in the roof and instructs those who are trimming and nailing shingles for the roof. There is a constant banter of cajoling, prodding, encouraging, and modeling. He could do it himself more quickly and with greater precision. But the yurt isn't what is most important; rather, it is the learning that takes place in those who create a new shelter. The completed yurt is a delight of functionality and beauty.

The yurt also represents a key element in Bill's educa-tional philosophy: that the highest forms of knowledge combine wisdom from many different cultures—all the more essential now that knowledge, skills, crafts, and arts are being threatened as local cultures are destroyed. "Cultural blending," he states, " has been an operating force in human affairs since one tribe first met with another. . . . If it should be true that folk wisdom is our basic wealth, the chief insurance of a culture, then we are nearly bankrupt. This knowledge is disappearing at an accelerating rate. . . .We need to be collecting as many examples as possible of the old knowledge and skill, before they are forgotten and lost forever."

At Bill's homestead, cultural blending is embedded in his life practice. He explains:

My house has its origins in the steppes of Asia. My felt boots came by way of Finland from Asian shepherds. My cucumbers came from Egypt, my lilacs from Persia, my boat from Norway, and my canoe is American Indian. My crooked knife for

themselves for material gain, while remaining provincial and violent. Democracy had become a system in which the many were manipulated by the few. Yet slowly it became clear to me that the basic human stock was sound and that the "democracy" I saw was not democracy but a distortion of it. As I became aware of our untapped potential as human beings, I began to grow in optimism and belief in our latent ability to solve problems. . . . Only a minute percentage of our abilities has been developed. . . . [I was not] concerned with what economic, political, or social system is best. I [was] concerned with education—the development of human beings, their growth.

paddle making is Bering Coast Eskimo, my axe is nineteenth-century Maine design, and my pick-up is twentieth-century Detroit. We are a cultural blend.

NONVIOLENCE

In the summer of 1955, when he traveled to Mexico as part of his graduate study, the disparate ideas that Bill Coperthwaite had encountered as a student crystallized into a specific vision of education and a way of living. "Things came together," Bill recalled, "when my appendix ruptured." A long hospital stay and recovery in Mexico allowed him to step back from his searching to reflect on all he had learned and encountered. Bill recalls:

There was absolutely no way, that I could see, that society could avert catastrophe. Everywhere there was pollution of air, water, minds; everywhere there was crime, poverty, political corruption, war, land and food poisoning. . . . I viewed the mass of humanity as easily duped, with people willing to sell

During the Korean War, Bill claimed conscientious objector status. For his alternative service, he was assigned to work with the American Friends Service Committee, which brought him back to Mexico. During this time Bill discovered the writings of Richard Bartlett Gregg (1885–1974). Gregg, a key figure in American pacifism, articulated a life practice of nonviolence connected to an expansive definition of democracy. "It was he who brought me closer to natural living, to Gandhi's work, to nonviolence, to simplicity. When I was hard put to find support for my beliefs, he encouraged me."

Bill found in Gregg's work reinforcement for his own application of philosophy to personal practice. As Gregg wrote in *The Power of Non-Violence*, and in the pamphlet that accompanied the book, *Training for Peace* (1937), "Non-violent resistance is not an evasion of duty to the state or the community. On the contrary, it is an attempt to see that duty in its largest and the most permanent and responsible aspect."

Richard Gregg had trained as a lawyer in the early years

of the twentieth century and graduated from Harvard Law School. He spent a number of years teaching and practicing corporate law before focusing his attention on industrial relations. In 1921, Gregg represented the Federation of Railway Shop Employees during a nationwide strike, an experience that shook his faith in the ideals of American democracy and led to his reconsideration of labor and class relations. During the strike he also encountered the writings of Mahatma Gandhi. As Gregg later described the moment, "At the height of the nationwide American railway strike of 1921, when feelings were most intense and bitter, I happened by pure chance to pick up in a Chicago bookshop a collection of Mahatma Gandhi's writings. His attitudes and methods were in such profound and dynamic contrast to what I was in the midst of then, that I felt impelled to go and live alongside of him and learn more."

Gregg left the United States for India in 1924 and would not return for four years, spending seven months at Gandhi's ashram. He studied Gandhi's philosophy and its application in all aspects of life. Gregg was the first American to popularize nonviolent resistance in the United States. While Gregg's influence is largely overlooked today, his writings were enormously influential in translating nonviolent resistance into modern Western concepts and terminology. *The Power of Non-Violence* was a handbook for resisters in the civil rights and peace movements of the 1950s and '60s and directly shaped the thinking of leaders in these movements. Martin Luther King, Jr., wrote to Gregg in 1959, "I don't know when I have read anything that has given the idea of non-violence a more realistic and depthful interpretation. I assure you that it will be a lasting influence in my life." The imprint of Gandhi's influence on Bill Coperthwaite can also be found along the path that runs through Gregg.

By the early 1950s, Gregg had relocated to Jamaica, Vermont, and become a close friend of economist and social activist Scott Nearing, who along with his wife, Helen, would become one of the leaders in a nationwide "back-to-the-land" movement. Gregg and Scott Nearing shared many interests and causes, and friendship was a natural outcome of their radical ideas and politics. With Nearing's help, Gregg built a small stone cabin high on the slope in the sugarbush behind the Nearings' homestead.

This was before the publication of Scott and Helen Nearing's book, *Living the Good Life* (1954), and Bill Coperthwaite would not encounter Nearing or his writings for years to come.

"I am concerned," Bill wrote, "as to how we can apply the Gandhian concept of nonviolence to life in this society. At the same time I am troubled that we tend to hear only Gandhi's words on nonviolence and fail to read the next line or page, which says that it is only one part in a complex of things, that there can be no nonviolent society without bread labor, decentralization, voluntary poverty, and the development of the whole person." In Bill's reading of Gandhi, this framework of nonviolent democracy also compels each of us as an American citizen to accept global responsibilities. "In this country we have a tremendous responsibility to the rest of the world," Bill counsels, "for whether we like it or not, and whether loved or hated, as the case may be, the world at large is following our lead toward greater industrialization, urbanization, and mobility, with the increasing impersonalization of life that these bring. We are obliged to find a way of life worth following, a way that encourages the best in man to unfold."

Gregg's *The Power of Non-Violence* resonated so strongly with Bill that he wrote to the author, initiating a correspondence that led to a lifelong friendship. He even hitchhiked from Mexico to New York and Gregg drove

Richard Gregg (left) and Scott Nearing at Jamaica, Vermont, in the early 1950s. (Photo by Rebecca Lepkoff, courtesy of The Thoreau Institute at Walden Woods.)

from Vermont to pick him up. Bill reflects, "We first met [when] I was twenty-five and he was nearly seventy. In his writing I had found a kindred spirit and so sought him out to thank him. It turned out [to be] a joyous event. Age difference seemed of no consequence. It was exciting to find that this gentle, white-haired man, with such wide knowledge of the world, had long before discovered many of the things that I was finding true in my world— the joy of bread labor; the importance of hands in education; simple living; the wonders of the technology of early peoples; and the relationship of these to nonviolence."

After finishing his alternative service and teaching for two years at North Country School, Bill headed south again in 1959, to Venezuela this time, to work on a rural development study for the Venezuelan government. When he returned to the States in 1960, he bought land in Maine, near the town of Machias, along the furthermost northeast reaches of the coast. He spent two years teaching at the Meeting School in Rindge, New Hampshire. He traveled to northern Scandinavia to study village culture and crafts, spending two years living among the Lapp people and learning their culture.

In 1966, Bill drove from Maine to Alaska to visit Eskimo villages and study their handcrafts and tools. During that trip he conceived the idea for a museum of Eskimo culture that would travel from village to village so that youth would be exposed to the arts and traditions they were rapidly losing. He submitted this project to the doctoral program of the Harvard Graduate School of Education and completed his dissertation about his Alaskan work.

SIMPLE LIVING

For Bill Coperthwaite, the practice of simple living has economic, social, and political implications. In this dimension, Bill was to find co-conspirators in Scott and Helen Nearing, who had commenced a more than fifty-year experiment in self-reliant homesteading and simple living.

Before leaving Depression-era New York City to move to Vermont, Nearing had spent decades developing a clearly defined personal philosophy and expressing it through active political dissent and protest. He wrote pamphlets and made speeches, engaged in civil disobedience, and ran for public office. He endured arrests, legal persecution (he was indicted under the Espionage Act in 1918), and firings (from two universities). Nearing was the embodiment of an extreme and pure form of noncooperation, living according to deeply held moral beliefs and exemplifying the position that how one lives is fundamentally a political act.

Nearing's politics of simple living are rooted in his early life as an economics professor at the University of Pennsylvania—from which he was fired in 1915 for denouncing child labor and advocating the redistribution of income—and elaborated in his subsequent efforts to be financially and materially self-sufficient as a homesteader. At the heart of Nearing's pursuits is the principle of non-exploitation and a commitment to social justice. Outrage over the exploitation of children that Nearing expressed in his 1911 book, *The Solution of the Child Labor Problem*, finds a corresponding expression, decades later, in a carefully developed practice of simple living that assiduously avoided exploitation of humans, animals, and the land. The Nearings created a way to live out their ethical and political logic through pacifism, vegetarianism, and environmentalism. As Scott and Helen wrote in *Living the Good Life* (1954), "We desire to liberate ourselves from the cruder forms of exploitation; the plunder of the planet, the slavery of man and beast, the slaughter of men in war, and animals for food." The Nearings' half-century of homesteading represents not an "exit strategy" from the complexities and contradictions of American culture, but a means of actively provoking genuine social change.

Bill Coperthwaite did not meet Scott Nearing until 1963. He avoided visiting the man about whom he had heard so much from Morris Mitchell and Richard Gregg, and whose books he had devoured, because he knew that the Nearings were inundated with visitors and seekers. It wasn't until Bill had published his letter in *Manas* magazine describing an alternative design for a school that he received a letter from Scott inviting him to the Nearing homestead in Harborside, Maine. They became good friends.

Bill Coperthwaite was drawn to Nearing's complex understanding of simple living, stressing the vital connections in everyday life between public and private, individual and community, personal and political. Bill also admired this teacher who, like Morris Mitchell, worked with head as well as hands, connecting theory and practice, nature and culture, human and nonhuman, labor and leisure, intellect and spirit, knowledge and ethics.

"Each time we learn to live more simply," Bill explains, "we aid the world in two ways: (1) We use less of the world's resources for our own life; (2) We help set an example for others who are now striving to copy the affluent life of their neighbors. The greater the striving for affluence, the more wretched will be the poor, and the greater will be the chasm between the haves and the have-nots. Violence will be inevitable.... Not only do we need to simplify in order to be able to share more of the things the world needs, but we need to distribute power, authority, and freedom as well. The more decentralized we become, the more opportunity will there be for individual decision-making."

DEMOCRACY

Bill Coperthwaite defines democracy as active participation and active experimentation. He finds hope for the flowering of democracy in the possibility that each individual can regain agency in his or her own life. But agency and experimentation *for what?* The promise of democracy can be betrayed by savage inequalities that mock the highest ideals. In a false democracy, individuals become only spectators to their own experience and to the wider intellectual, civic, and social life around them. "The work of creating a new society" can only be accomplished, according to Bill, through citizen action; not "by specialists, but by the people themselves to fit their needs." Only with "the encouragement to all people to take part" in exercising their "rights and obligations in designing the work of the future—discovering that their efforts are truly desired and needed—only then can a true democracy exist."

Bill's life represents a determined refutation of a culture of retreat. The widespread retreat from participation and direct experience tends to limit political action to a narrow definition of procedural democracy, the so-called electoral-representative process. This retreat makes protest, direct action, and mass involvement increasingly unlikely and ineffective.

Bill sees democratic action as that in which private behavior is recognized to have civic consequences. Here is a way of life that continuously asks the question, "How can I live according to what I believe?" Wendell Berry has described this kind of politics as "more complex and permanent, public in effect but private in its implementation." According to Berry:

To make public protests against an evil, and yet live dependent on and in support of a way of life that is the source of the evil, is an obvious contradiction and a dangerous one. If one disagrees with the nomadism and violence of our society, then one is under an obligation to take up some permanent dwelling place and cultivate the possibility of peace and harmlessness in it. If one deplores the destructiveness and wastefulness of the economy, then one is under an obligation to live as far out on the margin of the economy as one is able: to be as economically independent of exploitative industries, to learn to need less, to waste less, to make things last, to give up meaningless luxuries, to understand and resist the language of salesmen and public relations experts, to see through attractive packages, to refuse to purchase fashion or glamour or prestige. If one feels endangered by meaninglessness, then one is under an obligation to refuse meaningless pleasures and to resist meaningless work, and to give up the moral comfort and the excuses of the mentality of specialization.

In his book about the lives of homesteaders Harlan and Anna Hubbard, Berry tells a story of the politics of personal responsibility exemplified by Bill Coperthwaite, as well. In the mid-1970s, across the Ohio River from the Hubbards' homestead on the Kentucky side, Public Service Indiana began constructing a nuclear power plant. Berry joined with others who were concerned about the environmental impact of the plant. They organized protests, demonstrated, wrote letters, and engaged in a nonviolent sit-in at the site. Construction of the plant was never completed.

The Hubbards, to Berry's initial disappointment, never took part in the protests, never signed a letter, never spoke out. Yet in rethinking his understanding of their political impact, Berry realized that "by the life they led, Harlan and Anna had opposed the power plant longer than any of us.... They were opposed to it because they were opposite to it, because their way of life joined them to everything in the world that was opposite to it." As Berry asks, "What could be more radically or effectively opposite to a power plant, than to live abundantly with no need for electricity?" Berry's realization is illuminating as we consider the life of Bill Coperthwaite.

Bill lives close to the land in a forested coastal area of eastern Maine, heating with wood, eschewing grid electricity and plumbing and motors, and experimenting with nonviolent crafts and cultural practices. His democracy of one is not lived for himself alone. Bill has undertaken his way of life as an experiment that can have resonance for others, offering possibilities for a truer democracy in the future.

The Fallacy of Discipleship

Defining democratic life as a process of direct individual experience grants extraordinary significance to the importance of experimentation. There is no blueprint, no formula, and no set answers. Such a process of dynamic experimentation needs to be rooted in a specific place to be viable. In Bill Coperthwaite's life, that place is a coastal forest with a cleared meadow that sweeps down a slope marked at one end by a three-story yurt and bounded at the other by the water's edge in a tidal cove. His homestead is a compound of multiple buildings and trails, a rope swing, a tree house, and several canoes. Paramount to Bill's life is his long-term commitment and formal obligation to this place.

Also paramount is a lifelong commitment to independence in thought and action. He once wrote to a friend, "If we become mere followers of the great, we will get a collapsed society and a sterile ecosystem. We cannot afford to invest in followers. If a good society is to emerge on this planet, it will be through the efforts of creative, caring people. Let's invest all we have in finding and encouraging them. . . . We need not more disciples but more apprentices."

Discipleship lends itself to emulation or worship, preventing us from seeing through the lives of others into the possibilities for ourselves. The lesson of Bill Coperthwaite's life is a lesson of experimentation and apprenticeship, of independence of thinking and respect for those who have come before us, of commitment to future generations. "Can we think of this treasure as the fuel for the fire of truth? May we now be reaching the kindling point for the treasure? With creative ability of the minds of people now living, coupled with the wisdom developed over the centuries, we may create a self-sustaining flame of human happiness and growth."

This book, a richly textured exploration of Bill Coperthwaite's work and thought, encourages us to take the lessons of his life to heart. Each of us has the potential to craft our own lives with our own hands—actively, joyfully, and nonviolently, drawing upon the wisdom of our ancestors, striving for justice in the present, and fulfilling our obligations to those who will inherit our legacy.

John Saltmarsh is the author of *Scott Nearing: The Making of a Homesteader* (Chelsea Green, 1998)

A HANDMADE LIFE

*A*t every crossway on the road that leads to the future, each progressive spirit is opposed by a thousand men appointed to guard the path. Let us have no fear lest their fair towers of former days be sufficiently defended. The least that the most timid of us can do is not to add to the tremendous dead weight that nature drags along.

Let us not say to ourselves that the best truth always lies in moderation, in the decent average. The average, the decent moderation of today, will be the least human of things tomorrow. At the time of the Spanish Inquisition, the opinion of good sense and of the good medium was certainly that people ought not to burn too large a number of heretics; extreme and unreasonable opinion obviously demanded that they burn none at all.

Let us think of the great invisible ship that carries our human destinies upon eternity. Like the vessels of our confined oceans, she has her sails and her ballast. The fear that she may pitch and roll upon leaving the roadstead is no reason for increasing the ballast by stowing the fair white sails in the depths of the hold. They were not woven to molder side by side with the cobblestones in the dark. Ballast exists everywhere; all the pebbles of the harbor, all the sands of the beach will serve for that. But sails are rare and precious things; their place is not in the murk of the well but amid the light of the tall masts, where they will collect the winds of space.

—Maeterlinck

Who has not found the Heaven—below—
Will fail of it above—
For angels rent the house next ours,
Wherever we remove—

—Emily Dickinson

SOCIETY BY DESIGN / DESIGN BY SOCIETY

My heaven home is here,
No longer need I wait
To cross the foaming river
Or pass the pearly gate.

I've angels all around me,
With kindness they surround me,
To a glorious cause they've bound me,
My heavenly home is here.

—Shaker hymn

I who had sought afar from earth
The fairyland to meet
Now find content within its girth
And wonder nigh my feet . . .

And all I thought of heaven before
I find in earth below
A sunlight in the hidden core
To dim the noonday glow

And with the earth my heart is glad
I move as one of old
With mists of silver I am clad
And bright with burning gold.

—A.E. (George Russell)

For all too long we have had a society designed by Happenstance. There are simply too many losers, which is inefficient and uneconomical from any point of view.

We need to build a society in which everyone wins. Losers are not good for business. The cost of having so many losers is tremendous in terms of happiness; in dollars for health care, famine relief, and prisons; in suffering and in wars—in wasted human potential.

We have the knowledge and resources to raise the well-being of all to unheard-of heights. We have in our hands the potential to create a blossoming of human culture—an Eden on earth and in the minds of human beings.

Will we be able to do it? Can we find the will to do it? For me, this is a design problem.

EDEN, HERE AND NOW

When I was a child, the word "design" meant to me something far off in a world where artists lived. Growing older, the word slipped a notch in my regard, as I came to think of design as a surface treatment—superficial, often cosmetic—cheap and gaudy, the dazzle aimed at conning a buyer. I was no longer in awe of the word but disdained it.

Then, observing the world more closely, I began to feel that this sense of the word was a misuse of the term by the commercial world. Design gradually came to mean to me that certain quality whereby a well-shaped spoon works. I began to find good design in quality work everywhere—in Finnish log houses, Dutch windmills, Eskimo fishhooks, Indian moccasins, Swampscot dories.

Here was a joyous discovery. One of the most important qualities of life, that conscious shaping toward perfection, now had a name: design.

Still, the word's connotations clung to the world of things. But as my concern for society and my understanding of its needs grew, I found myself reaching out for a phrase to convey the concept of a new form of education, and I began to think in terms of educational design. This idea grew into broader thoughts of family design, community design, and eventually life design, meaning the logical shaping of one's own life. All this thinking finally knit itself together under one term—social design.

"Design" had now come full circle from my childhood, when I had associated the word with something especially beautiful, wondrous, marvelous. So "design," as used here, implies not only beauty, well formed for use, but includes also the aspect of active human shaping for positive ends.

Good design is one of the most critical needs at this point in human history, not only practiced by those who are called designers but by society as a whole. We need a wider awareness of the need for good design in all elements of life, and we need to encourage all people to take part. The finest design for society will not be one worked up by specialists but a design created by the people themselves to fit their needs. Planners and designers are needed, but to help, not to preempt, the democratic work of creating a new society.

Only as all members of society become aware of their right and obligation to take part in designing the world of the future—and comprehend the need for everyone to take part, knowing that their efforts are truly welcome and necessary—only then can a genuine democracy exist.

Everyday Adventure

For many in our society life is pallid, dull, and insipid, lacking in any sense of adventure. How can we develop in our young the sense of wonder, of magical beauty in living and learning? A sense of excitement and eagerness to learn is natural in all children, yet we have found ways to stifle these enthusiasms in a very effective manner.

If we could be as efficient in supporting a child's eagerness to learn as we have been in stifling this eagerness, this would revolutionize life as we know it.

This is one of the key questions pertaining to the improvement of human welfare: How can we build excitement and meaning into daily life—not with motorcycles, tennis, and TV, but with socially valid action?

Seldom are the young people in our society helped to see the ways in which they can be useful, experiencing the joys of working together. The Outward Bound movement takes its motto, "To seek, to serve, and not to yield," from Tennyson's poem "Ulysses": Outward Bound has demonstrated some very positive approaches to this problem in programs that get young people sailing, climbing, canoeing, and desert trekking. Yet one drawback of these programs is that they are only a three-to-four-week exception from the norm. What we need is to increase the sense of adventure in daily life, all year long.

To seek, to serve—
and be a little yielding ...

The Small and the Subtle

Nothing is too small or insignificant to be well designed. In the society I would like to see, no detail would be too insignificant to receive its due consideration. Whether we make or buy the things we need, paying attention to what is small and subtle can make a great deal of difference in the world around us.

And good design need not stop with tools, dishes, and houses—it can also include our selection of food, of friends, and of those who teach our children. We need to consider good design in relation to family, community, and school.

For example, think about our children's happiness. We

are continually constructing "better" school buildings, and yet we rarely take happiness into consideration. If we are going to have a better world, we need to insist that the finest people are selected for the care of the young. We must see that they get the status, recognition, and salary that will help draw people of the finest abilities into teaching.

Good design would mean allocating our money and prestige to people rather than buildings and gadgetry, which would result in not only a healthier and happier society but also better gadgets, better medicine, better politics, and better management.

I think we should reward those who work with the youngest children with the highest salaries of all. Do you want better doctors? Improve kindergarten.

SUCCESS

Is it possible to build a society in which all people are successful? Yes, if we define success not in terms of competition—where for one to succeed, another must fail—but in nonviolent terms, wherein success means universal growth, health, and maturity.

In our society competition gets better press than cooperation. Why this happens to be so, I do not know. Society is actually based on cooperation to a greater extent than on competition.

With the vast mental ability that we collectively possess, can we not develop a definition of success that will encourage each person to develop to the fullest of his or her capacity? The more people who become successful in this nonexploitative way, the more successful will be the society we live in, improving the quality of life for all of us.

Even in our highly competitive society, children absorbed in creation seem oblivious to their surroundings. Only after they have finished do they look about to see what others have done. Alas, that's when they so often begin to feel judgmental and self-conscious.

A number of years ago I took a traveling museum of Eskimo culture to Eskimo villages on the coast of the Bering Sea, with the purpose of giving the villagers a chance to see some of the beautiful examples of their culture that were hidden from them in museums. From December 1969 to April 1970, I visited twenty Eskimo villages and put on approximately seventy programs. To enable the Eskimo children to get into closer contact with the art of their people, we let each one choose a slide of an Eskimo print and project this onto a sheet of paper. They paired up to trace their images with felt-tipped pens, then laid the paper on the floor to color it. How delightful to see the beauty of their collaborations and the loveliness of the cooperative art the children produced.

SECURITY

If we are to design a world without violence and prejudice, we must develop ways to help people become more confident, aware, and secure. The less secure we are within ourselves, the greater our need to put others down—to try and make ourselves feel superior.

The Darwinian notion that ceaseless competition promoted the survival of the fittest individual has by now generally given way to the understanding that evolutionary success was due to the survival of the fittest community through interlocking cooperation.

—KIRKPATRICK SALE

"Birds Startled by Spirit," drawn by Lucy, colored by the children of Hooper Bay, Alaska.

Putting others down is a sick response, a blind, short-range, unhealthy response, increasing the likelihood that prejudice will be used on us in return. One way of helping build confidence and thus counter the spiral of violence in everyday life—which culminates in warfare—is to help others to gain a closer, more sensitive relationship with their environment. The resulting knowledge and sense of belonging are a strong antidote for insecurity.

It helps my thinking to imagine society as an extension of myself—as my social body. Anything I do to harm that body does harm to me. My neighbors' poverty is mine; their need is my need, as well. And all prejudice, all violence, all hatred that I send out into the world returns to me. John Donne crystallized this for us all by saying, ". . . any man's death diminishes me, because I am involved in mankinde; and therefore never send to know for whom the bell tolls; it tolls for thee."

Seeking the Right Distance

In everyday life, there is a great deal of unnecessary, avoidable friction and violence among people. One remedy—a design solution—is to look at the world differently.

For example, take the platitude that we should love all people. Love is often presumed to mean being close, in continual contact. Couples assume that they should want to be together all the time, and when they begin to dislike such constant closeness, they fear that some quality is lacking in the relationship.

Likewise, some "intentional communities" seek to live in togetherness and complete sharing, and when the members can't handle this they feel they have failed.

Or older couples, with happy lives and families behind them, will suddenly have more time together than before, and may find their spouse's nearness oppressive.

While the resulting separations might be blamed on lack of compatibility, sensitivity, and caring, the desire for more privacy is wholly normal under the circumstances. For any two people, there is an ideal distance in the relationship. This is like the attraction between two planets. At the proper distance they keep orbiting, but if they approach one another too closely, they collide, and if they get too far apart they drift away.

This is neither good nor bad, but simply the way things are.

Finding the right distance takes sensitivity and understanding on the part of each one in a relationship, and this ideal balance between intimacy and independence varies over time. Some people we can see once a year and have a delightful time, whereas twice a year would be wearing. Others we can meet weekly and enjoy a stimulating and mutually supportive relationship, but were we to share the same house the effect would be bedlam. Some people

D. Porter

can live extremely closely all their lives—working, eating, sleeping together. Others can reside happily together but need to work apart.

The newlyweds who understand this will realize the hazards of living too closely together, and instead of being threatened, they will happily seek the right distance in their relationship.

The community that recognizes this will likewise not be threatened but try to find the right spacing in its relationships and obligations. Often it is more effective to begin with more distance and to slowly come closer by degrees. The opposite approach of beginning relationships too near and adjusting by backing up seems to generate more hurt feelings, self-doubt, and insecurity.

Here is an opportunity to use the resources of good design. A couple coming to retirement knowing that changing circumstances will affect closeness and distance in their relationship can address the potential danger; they can avoid the pitfalls and rearrange their lives, seeking the needed balance. Recognizing such characteristics in human relating can lift the problem out of the emotional realm, removing the distractions of guilt and allowing us to rationally arrange the spaces in our lives for our mutual benefit.

But let there be space in your togetherness
And let the winds of heaven blow between you—
Sing and dance together and be joyous
But let each of you stand alone
Even as the strings of the lute are alone
Though they quiver with the same music.

—Kahlil Gibran

Every child has a right to a family with a purpose.
This is just as important as food and affection.
The members of the family do not necessarily do the
same work, yet they can be together in spirit,
united in a feeling of camaraderie and teamwork.

Homemaking

So much—words and conceptions—needs rethinking. So many of our values are dependent on the perspective of the times, which is often little more than a mix of passing fashions.

At the moment, throughout the United States, homemaking is looked down upon as a rather old-fashioned avocation. In reality, this is the most important profession and can be the most exciting of all.

It is sad that the true meaning of homemaking has been so misunderstood. In most communities it is now difficult for a young girl (to say nothing of a young boy) to grow up with the goal of becoming a homemaker. This prejudice has come about because some people have a bad experience with homemaking, feeling confined and circumscribed by the obligation to tend the home in lieu of a professional career. Without a doubt, any social institution can be misused.

Even so, a Turkish proverb says that it is shortsighted to burn your blanket to get rid of a flea. The home is our most important social realm, and unless we give the home the respect it is due and stop the incessant erosion now taking place, we will suffer irreparable loss.

The home is the center of education and emotional security, two of the essential elements of a healthy society. More and more, the functions of the home have been taken over by the school, but a school is no substitute for family, no matter how fine the instructors or expensive the equipment.

"The hand that rocks the cradle rules the world" is an avowal glibly repeated but given little heed. But the hand that rocks the cradle *does* rule the world, if not for good then for ill.

And unless the bearer of that hand perceives the honor, beauty, and responsibility of the role, the effect as often as not will be discord. There is no foundation more crucial than the sensitive care of the young in building a sane society. What mental insolvency has overtaken us that we can allow the core of our culture to be so denigrated and weakened? What a failure of design!

Far better to burn the house to the ground and live in a cave than lose your sense of wonder and privilege in making a home.

> We started leaving the home to go to work in order
> to support the home. We have been doing this
> for so long that we have forgotten the purpose
> for which we sold ourselves in the first place.

Cradling in New Traditions

The small farm family of a hundred years ago provided most human needs. People sold little for cash and bought little. Life was hard but in many cases happy.

As with Frost's two roads that diverged in a yellow wood, in advancing from those small farms we had two roads to choose between. One path was to abandon the farm and the skills of husbandry in favor of industrial development, allegedly to make life less hard physically. There was another path that could have been taken: we could have retained our homestead life, with its tremendous potential for human development, and applied our scientific and technological skills to make life on the homestead easier and less isolated. Now some in this country are moving in that direction, not back to an antiquated way of life but forward to a blend of the best of the past with the best of today.

It is with such blending that social design is concerned. Not "back to the land" but "down to earth."

For emotional stability we need traditions to lean on. The extent to which we can alter our customs and still feel emotionally secure is probably quite small. Many people evidently relish change, but we change too many traditions at our peril.

This does not mean that when we see an unhealthy tradition (such as going to war) that we must accept it; but for all traditions we deplore and wish to change, there are myriad others that give us comfort and continuity.

As traditions are so helpful in innumerable unseen ways, we need to design society in a way that gives positive traditions emphasis.

In an ideal society we would continue to see the young rebelling against traditions, even these positive traditions, which later, upon more mature reflection, the former rebels would find valid.

> Have you considered the most essential geographical
> factors in your child's life, or in your own?
> What is most important in your lives: The land?
> The sea? The sky? The desert? The forest? Or is it the
> convenience store? The sidewalk? The parking lot?
> The highway? The TV set? So often a house is chosen for
> its neighborhood, for its nearness to a good school,
> or for the social status it carries. Imagine
> how fine it would be instead to choose a special tree
> or a stream for your "comforting neighbor." Why not
> resolve to be near a certain hill, a grove of trees,
> some handsome ledges, or a giant boulder standing
> up to the sky, and then design and build a home
> that fits both you and the surroundings?

Folk Ways and "Health Foods"

Designing a new culture is inevitably a self-conscious process, not without risks of excess. An example of the danger in creating a self-conscious culture to take the place of a culture supported by folk ways is our present, notably self-conscious concept of diet.

As we've lost an understanding of healthy traditional sources of nutrition, modern people are left to their own guesswork to decide what represents a balanced meal. But the resulting judgments are seldom adequate and, considering the impact of slanted advertising, are rarely our own.

Under pressure of marketing, and the widespread poisoning of land and food with "preservatives" and "fertilizers," the average person has little chance of choosing sensibly. The only alternative seems to be to become very self-conscious about food. By this means some few people learn to live healthily, while a great many others go to extremes—all carrot juice, or no bread, or all brown rice and no dairy products.

It is nearly impossible for a society to acquire a naturally healthy diet without guidance from traditions. We need, therefore, to carefully examine our traditions and keep the best of them in practice.

I would by no means argue that all folk diets are good, but learning to create a well-designed diet that in time becomes traditional would correct the excesses and oscillations of today's self-conscious food fads. Who has time to measure every calorie, test for every vitamin?

But for a new traditional diet to come into being will require redesigning the care of our land, soil, and animals, as well as our legal and moral codes, which even with supposedly good intentions are quite unable to halt the adulteration and poisoning of foods.

We run risks in self-consciously re-designing our family life, our houses, and our communities, but we have no choice. With all our shortcomings, we must apply conscious effort to the improvement of life for all, with the hope that our efforts, applied over a long enough time, will result in designs that provide a sound base for future tradition.

Encouragement

The main thrust of my own work is not "simple living," not yurt design, not even "social design," although each of these has importance and receives large contributions of my time.

Yet my central concern is *encouragement*—encouraging people to seek, to experiment, to design, to create, and to dream.

The only hope I see for our survival is to encourage the fullest development of all minds. Safety, truly, lies in numbers. One of these minds may find a brilliant solution, but even more certain, when we have more minds concerned, any challenge shrinks proportionally. The solution to our greatest problems may simply be involvement.

In the past, we looked to experts, to leaders, to national heroes for knowledge and guidance. To continue doing so means accepting a paternalistic way of life that holds us in a state of permanent adolescence.

And deferring to the experts is tremendously wasteful, stifling the imagination. We deny ourselves the joy of full development at a time when we're in need of all the creativity we can muster to solve the desperate problems confronting our world. All these leaders and planners, however wise and skillful they may be, are simply no match for the challenge.

As an analogy, think of a child lost in a forest. We can send out an expert. A good tracker, given enough time, might find the child, but perhaps it will be too late. One person can't cover enough ground. Instead, we recruit as many people as possible, as quickly as possible, to comb the countryside.

Expert knowledge is certainly needed in every area, but too little concern has been given to the value of stumbling. If enough people are searching—stumbling as they may—we will make many discoveries, and the stumbling diminishes as our searching skills get honed with practice. There is also great value in all of us realizing that our efforts are worthwhile, that we are needed, and that our abilities can be improved with use.

We need to design our responses to society's emergencies to involve as many people as possible, and not be afraid of some inevitable stumbling.

I remember a time in my life, about fifty years ago, when after growing aware of the state of the world, I became greatly depressed. There was absolutely no way I could see that society would avert catastrophe. Nearly everywhere there was pollution of air, water, and minds; there was crime, poverty, political corruption, war, and poisoning of land and food. I viewed the mass of humanity as easily duped, with people willing to sell themselves for material gain while remaining provincial and violent. Democracy had become a system in which the many were manipulated by the few.

Yet slowly it became clear to me that the basic stock of humanity was sound, although the "democracy" I saw around us was not democracy at all but a distortion. As I became more aware of our untapped potential as human beings, I began to grow in optimism and belief in our latent ability to solve our problems.

I continue to feel that only a minute percentage of our potential has been developed. I am not concerned here with what economic, political, or social system is best. I am concerned with education—the full development of human beings.

> The goal of social design is to improve the quality of life on earth. The greatest hurdle is disbelief in our own potential—learning to believe we can design and build a better world.

> If we can find ways to help one another—especially our young—grow to full, sensitive, creative adulthood, we will not need to concern ourselves with what specific style of government or economic system we need. The coming generation will be so much better equipped that they will be able to design the new institutions and ways of life needed.

FINE THINGS

Most of us enjoy having fine things. How we define "fine" is going to affect greatly whether we live lives of quiet exploitation or of fairness.

For instance, having a fine house can be a matter of status, of expense and extravagance, or it can mean having the best house for you and your needs, a home that you design and build, a home that is fine because it is simply just right.

Having nice things does not have to mean having expensive things. The quality of a thing comes from the knowledge and beauty it carries more than from its expense. Having one of the best pancake-turners in the world is possible for anyone who finds out what constitutes a good pancake-turner. Money need not enter into the equation.

If you put many such small, incremental elements together, you can create one of the finest homes possible.

It is these little elements multiplied many times over

I am done with great things and big things, great institutions and big success, and I am for those tiny invisible molecular moral forces that work from individual to individual by creeping through the crannies of the world like so many rootlets, or like the capillary oozing of water, yet which, if you give them time, will rend the hardest monuments of man's pride.

—William James

that make up our daily world. The impact of subtleties upon the quality of our life and work is incalculable. And the more that good design surrounds us, the easier it becomes to design well. Remember, the chief elements in good design are sensitivity and care; expense is a relatively minor factor.

The concept of social design implies change—the rebuilding or reshaping of something, a process of transformation. Imagine what would happen if three hundred million people were concerned with building a better world! This would be a social revolution such as never before. The key difference between such a massive awakening and our present circumstances would be the realization on the part of huge numbers of people that this is *their* world: that the world *can* be changed, and that they *can, should,* and *must* have a role in redesigning that world.

For this to occur, designing would need to become like reading and writing, eating and sleeping, normal and familiar to everyone.

Design By and For Machine

Of course, the end result of a better world will be as much a consequence of the process of seeking as it is an outcome of specific design ideas.

And unless design becomes the shared imaginative domain of all, we will continue to be exploited by the designers dedicated to commercial interests.

An aware public cannot be sold shoddy goods, ranging from tableware that is hard to wash because of "floral" ornaments and school programs that do not foster education, to nuclear power plants that cannot be accommodated by the environment and wars intended to "save us from our enemies."

We are constantly manipulated by design. Industrial production has been a boon in providing many needed things at a lower cost, but unless we are alert we'll let the machine start teaching us design. For instance, machines can be used to create any form of chair we like, but commercial interests can make more chairs (and more money) if the simplest design *for the machines* is chosen for production. So we end up surrounded by furniture designed to fit the needs of machines.

An example is the commercial slat-back chair with turned legs and rungs and a woven bottom. This chair has been made by machine for so long that it has become the norm for its type. But the person who wants to make such a chair by hand rarely questions the need for a lathe. It is possible to build a perfectly good chair with no lathe—the "rounds" do not need to be round or turned. All the necessary parts can be shaped with a knife, an axe, or a draw knife. Yet industrial production has so controlled the design of chairs that we now have a difficult time imagining how the form might differ if a chair were handmade.

A Choice of Engines

Once or twice a week, I go forty minutes by canoe to get supplies. Some people think it strange that I don't use a motor and thereby do the trip in fifteen or twenty minutes.

I enjoy the paddle. This excursion is one of the most relaxing and thought-provoking times of the week. I not only can see an osprey flying, I can hear it. And the exercise feels good. I have no argument with the use of motors, but they are not applicable in all situations. They are not a *better* way to move about, just *another* way.

As I write I can hear the deep throb of a lobster boat coming to haul traps in the bay. The engine makes good sense, in the right place. To tend four hundred traps a power boat is a necessity, but to tend five traps it's a bit ridiculous. As with everything, a sense of proportion is necessary.

We need to design and select tools to fit our specific needs, and we need to select and design a technology to fit society as a potter fits a glaze to a bowl. In many cases, a technology that was designed for mass production is not

well suited to a homestead. Likewise, agribusiness techniques are not needed or appropriate in the home garden. A table saw is not a necessity for making a cedar chest. And I can't think of anything more ridiculous than an electric can opener.

In Search of Keys

The world is in such a crisis that we need to seek out key areas on which to focus our attention.

Keys work like catalysts, whereby a small amount of effort brings about a large result. We need to locate, define, and concentrate on areas wherein a modest initial effort will effect a broad and positive social change.

In our prejudice, our nationalisms, our violation of minds in schools and jobs, and our distorting of minds and bodies through industry and warfare, we have proof that our present-day "managers" are incapable of designing a fully productive, healthy, and happy society. When we reach social maturity, our citizens will do their own thinking and designing, no longer delegating that role.

If I appear to discount or underestimate the value of experts here, my apologies. Experts are needed as never before. But only by complete and genuine development of our whole people will we find the raw material we need to transform the world.

And a word of respect is due for an ancient kind of expert, the sages. Often their knowledge is of a general nature, gained in breadth of perspective over time. They continue to have much wisdom to share.

One contribution they make is encouragement. Inspiration is as vital as knowledge. Support from those who have gone before provides a special sustenance. In searching for a solid footing from which to approach the task of social design, my life is greatly indebted to the encouragement and example of several sages, old as well as wise.

Dead Time

"Why not get some horses?"
Comes over the water,
From a 30-foot lobster boat
With 300 horses,
To my 20-foot canoe with
A one-man cedar engine.

It's a two-mile paddle to haul supplies
By rock-bound shore and gnarled spruce.
Osprey "float" above with sharp cries.
A startled heron croaks displeasure
Waiting for the tide to drop.
If lucky—there may be otter kits
Playing in the shallows
At the tide rips.
An eagle perches on a snag,
Loon laughter lilts over the long bay,
A seal looks me over.

A motor would take half the time—
But, what with mounting it,
Feeding it, and keeping it in tune,
Would there really be a gain in time?
True—I could go when the wind is
Too strong to paddle
But that is a non-problem.

The racket, the stench, the poisons—
There is the problem.
Oh—I could still see (most of) the birds
But not hear them
And the otters—they'd be long gone.

The paddle—lovely yellow cedar—
Carved on a beach in the San Juans,
Has served me well these thirty years.

While paddling the brain does delightful things,
Each moment a surprise—a treasure.
Motoring puts all that on hold,
Thieving those precious minutes—
My brain turned off:
Dead time.

I have long admired certain communities for their design of a common life, the Shakers and Doukhobors, in particular. Yet rather than defining solutions for the present according to Shaker and Doukhobor ways, chiefly I value these older models for the way they stimulate and challenge us to go further.

Those who guide us, who inspire us, having gone our way before, are now partners with us in building a better world. Any success we have is theirs as well as ours. To copy or imitate them should be only the beginning—the apprentice stage of life. It is fine to think, "What would a Shaker do? What would Scott Nearing have said? What would Gandhi have thought?" These are good exercises for the mind, a way of weighing ideas and contemplated actions, valuable so long as we do not follow anyone blindly.

Only by standing on their shoulders can we build a better world, but we should use the wise as advisers, not masters.

Learning to walk requires some stumbling
and falling.

Apprentices Needed, Not Disciples

For many, the knowledge of a Jesus, a Lao-tzu, a Buddha, or a Gandhi is complete and unassailable. But we do them and their vision a disservice when we follow them rather than using what they have taught to build upon as we strive toward our goal of a better society.

When we merely follow another, we take a potentially creative mind out of service—our own. We tie up a natural resource, just as much as when we put away money in the mattress.

We don't need more disciples, we need more apprentices, the difference being that an apprentice serves as a follower only temporarily and is expected to go on and work independently. Wise apprentices recognize that the masters are always a part of them, that within them is a partnership of apprentice and master artisan, including all the other masters that came before.

Good apprentices know that they are in the process of becoming masters and that as responsible artisans they must seek to improve upon the knowledge entrusted to them and go further.

As apprentices we are not better than those who went before. We are a part, an extension of our predecessors, the newest buds on an ancient, living tree. If we do not reach up to the sun and down into the soil for nourishment to help the tree grow, we have not been faithful to the trust invested in us.

It is always easier to take the words of a Jesus, a Gandhi, a Marx, or a Confucius as constituting Holy Writ. This involves less reading, less study, less thought, less conflict, and less independent searching, but it also means less growth toward maturity.

Cultural Parentage

There are many kinds of seeds in each of us. Usually we think in terms of a person's genetic inheritance. I like to think in terms of cultural parentage, of intellectual inheritances—the ideas and values bequeathed to us. Perhaps it is good to ask ourselves: "Who are my brothers and my sisters?"*

We have known in our era a number of brilliant minds, flowers on the tree of human knowledge. Eric Fromm is one example, Carl Rogers is another, and still another is Abraham Maslow. These people were not followers. They

---

*My answer is: *My brothers and sisters are quoted throughout this book.*

brought new knowledge, deep-rooted in the wisdom of the past, from many sources.

We need knowledge brought forward from the past, collected, studied, experimented with, and blended together with modern knowledge for the creation of a new culture. Cultural blending has been an operating force in human affairs since one tribe first met with another.

Learning from one another is natural. Each group of people in the world is a repository of folk knowledge that is their inheritance from previous generations. Such knowledge is a valuable resource for all of humanity. Whether this be knowledge of child care, gardening, human relations, or tool design, such knowledge needs to be gathered and studied for its value in blending with other knowledge from other cultures.

Folk wisdom is often rare and unique, vitally necessary as we work at building a new world. And folk ways are of even greater value when they are learned from a living culture. Besides the value to us of what we learn, there is a value to them in feeling that their way of life has something to contribute to humanity as a whole. When we learn from what others have to teach we grow in respect for them, increasing the feeling of the interdependency of all.

My house has its origins on the steppes of central Asia. My felt boots came by way of Finland from Asian shepherds. My cucumbers came from Egypt, my lilacs from Persia, my boat from Norway, and my canoe is American Indian. My crooked knife for paddle-making is Bering Coast Eskimo, my axe is a nineteenth-century Maine design, and my pickup is twentieth-century Detroit. The list is long. The more our knowledge increases, the greater becomes our awareness of indebtedness to others.

We are each a cultural blend. So why not recognize this truth and deliberately make use of the possibilities for a better way of life, whether in medicine, agriculture, child care, architecture, or a host of other areas?

LEARNING FIRSTHAND

If it is true that folk wisdom is our basic wealth, the chief insurance of a culture's worth, then we are nearly bankrupt. Traditional knowledge is disappearing at an accelerating rate, as the creations of local craftspeople are replaced by factory-made products, which are not designed with a concern for the improvement of human life but merely for profit. We need to be collecting as many examples as possible of the old knowledge and skill, before they are forgotten and lost forever.

Learning to plant a garden from a Mexican village family provides insight and perspective that has various ad-

---

There is no I
(except ego-centrically)
Only a wonderful
We

Part of me is Grandmother
Part Emily D.
Part Scott Nearing
(Who was part H.D.T.)
Part every person I've ever met
Whether in life or in lit.

'Tis delightful—being this blend—
This
We.

vantages over similar information obtained by reading a book. Living and working in the village, partaking of the whole atmosphere, may suggest new ways of using this knowledge when at home.

If we delegate such learning, we should be sure to select sensitive, observant, and empathetic researchers, because their inputs of thinking may make the knowledge gathered many times more useful.

We should also aim to do more than merely ape other cultures. Only through careful selection can we design a culture that fits our own particular needs.

Sitting on the floor may presently be a fad for Westerners. Yet there is something to be said for the simplicity of sitting on a chair or bench: you spend less energy getting up and down; and the floor is usually the coldest part of the room, so raised chairs and beds are sensible in a chilly climate.

Inflated seal skins make excellent boat rollers for an Eskimo, but they deteriorate rapidly where it is warmer, so we use their idea for our soft-tired vehicles but substitute rubber for seal skin, another cultural blend.

INTERDEPENDENCE

Have you ever known someone who, after cutting a finger or developing a blister, said: "Oh, it's nothing—it's just my

Years ago I began to recognize my kinship with all living beings, and I made up my mind that I was not one whit better than the meanest on earth. I said then, and I say now, that while there is a lower class, I am in it; while there is a criminal element, I am of it; while there is a soul in prison, I am not free.

—EUGENE V. DEBS

finger . . ."? Yet the finger is an essential part of the whole body, and through that finger the entire organism is impaired. Moreover, the whole organism assumes responsibility for healing the hurt part. Just as the finger is an extension of the physical body, so each of us is an extension of the social body. Whatever we do as individuals affects the whole, and what other individuals do affects us. These effects may not be visible for some time, as with a teredo worm boring into a ship's bottom, yet the results are no less real for being unseen at first. However small the individual holes, the ship will sink.

For me, one of the attributes of maturity is that we reach that stage when we act as though whatever happens to society happens to us. We will no longer feel good when we hear of the devaluation of the euro, the ruble, the peso. We, too, will feel the financial losses of people in other countries, knowing the suffering these changes bring. The waste of lives and minds because of poverty is my business, and yours. When a crime is committed, it is some part of our own social body which commits that crime.

War in Nigeria . . . It is *our* body that suffers there. Starvation in Bangladesh . . . It is *our* children who hunger. A riot in a distant city? That is *our* city, *our* heads being broken. Unemployment, welfare checks, slum conditions— all are ills of *our* body. If that small portion of the social body that I identify with locally is to stay healthy, I must work to see that the whole is healthy.

Enlightened Selfishness

We have been taught that "selfishness" is bad, and in general, this is a useful and necessary rule. As a society, we condemn selfishness as too great a concern for one's own being. Narrow, crabbed, ignorant selfishness hurts others and ourselves.

Yet this principle may be at odds with a more inclusive conception of the social body. Perhaps the problem is not selfishness, because it is normal for an organism to be concerned with its own welfare, but rather shortsighted or unenlightened selfishness that supposes it can achieve well-being at the expense of others.

When we see the social body as an extension of our-selves, narrow definitions of selfishness drop away. What we need is not less selfishness but a less narrow selfishness. We need selfishness that's enlightened, to the point where we see that our welfare is inextricably *intertwingled* with the welfare of all. Through enlightened selfishness I can recognize my neighbor's need as my own.

Our Common Inheritance

Down through the ages we have been gaining in knowledge, each generation standing on the shoulders of those who have gone before, and we have been coming closer and closer to launching into flight.

The prejudice and hatred that lead to war belong to the mixed-up adolescence of humanity. A mature society, like a mature human being, can recognize the tremendous advantages of cooperative effort over competition.

We are not wiser, we are not better, we are not stronger than our predecessors, but we have their accumulated knowledge and wisdom to build upon. We have gained in understanding and technical knowledge: this vast treasure house is our inheritance. With the creative intelligence of the people now living combined with wisdom developed over the centuries, we may create a self-sustaining flame of human happiness.

You say, "Isn't it sad that a diamond, when seen to its essence, is nothing but common carbon?" I say, "Isn't it wonderful that common carbon, in its most developed form, is the finest of diamonds?" You say, "Isn't it sad that altruism, when seen in its basic structure, is nothing but base selfishness?" I say, "Isn't it marvelous that base selfishness, in its most enlightened form, is the purest of altruism?"

—Pierre Ceresole

16

When love and skill work together, expect a masterpiece.

—John Ruskin

A Democratic Axe

It is hard to find a good broad hatchet—a small, broad axe with a wide cutting edge beveled on only one side, like a chisel; this special bevel makes it easier to hew to a line.

After forty years of hunting in antiques shops and flea markets, I have found only two broad hatchets that passed muster. To friends who sought one of their own, the outlook was discouraging. They could get one made—*if* they happened to know a good blacksmith, *if* they had a good design, and *if* they could afford the price.

Or you could forge one yourself, but by the time you had learned to make a fine one, you would have become a blacksmith yourself. This is an elite tool.

In Japan, in the Tosa region of the island of Shikoku, I was surprised by the number of blacksmiths. Each village had its smith, and all could make excellent edge tools. It was delightful to see the grace and skill of those smiths. I became friends with one who made a broad hatchet to my specifications. Twenty years went by, and in the interim I had studied many axes and was blending what I had

learned into my ideal of a broad hatchet.

A few years ago I carved a pine model and sent it off to my blacksmith friend in Shikoku. Yes, he would make it for me. Two years passed and it did not appear. I assumed the project was forgotten.

While visiting Italy, I came upon an elderly smith who had made axes years ago. I carved another pattern, and he forged the axe. Now, these are far from democratic tools. To get one you first have to design it and then know a smith in Japan or Italy or wherever who can—and is willing to—make an axe from your design.

It was doubtful that the axe from Japan would materialize, and the Italian smith was very old and sick and would probably not make another. A good broad hatchet for students and friends who wanted one was as elusive as ever. And though this axe adventure was exciting, and I had acquired some fine ones, we badly needed to have some inexpensive ones available.

While studying in Switzerland the breakthrough came.

The tiny fellow who lives upstairs above my right ear (and works mostly at night) shouted "Eureka!" He presented me with a full-blown design for a democratic axe.

I could hardly wait to get back to my bench. For steel there was an ancient plow point of about the right thickness lying behind the barn. Into the bonfire it went and when glowing red, we heaped ashes over it and let it remain until morning, cooling slowly and releasing its hardness. Next day I reheated and hammered it flat using a handy ledge for an anvil. When it cooled, I drew the pattern on it. Three hours of work at the vise was needed to cut it to shape with a hacksaw and another hour to dress it with files.

For us amateurs in axe making, there are two major difficulties. One of these is forging the eye of the axe—the hole into which the handle is inserted in a conventional axe. This democratic design eliminates the eye. The other difficulty is tempering, or bringing the steel to the correct hardness. Smiths have long been respected for their skill at this magical process of tempering steel, which requires good judgment and much experience to be able to do dependably.

After a good deal of pondering, experimenting, and reading all that I could find on tempering, some of the mystery began to fade. Before tempering, the steel must be hardened by being brought to red heat and then plunged in water. Then it seemed that tempering was merely a matter of temperature control. So we put the axe in an oven set at 475°F for half an hour and let it cool slowly. This worked!

Now, you smiths may object, reminding us that a tool like an axe that gets a blow needs to be soft in the eye to resist breaking. To this charge I plead *nolo contendere*. However, a broad hatchet is made with a short handle for use on a block, and such hatchets do not undergo the same severity of blows.

For the first time, we now have a democratic axe—an axe that most anyone who wants one can have. (You say you never knew you needed an axe, and I say, very well. Even so, here we have another example of one more democratic tool, which will make design of the next one a little easier, whatever its purpose.)

This experience with the broad hatchet is important for me on several levels. First it has been a exciting adventure all along the way, from learning to appreciate the variations in different forms of such a basic tool, to designing my own which others made, to ultimately making my own. Another level of the adventure is to be able to help others make their own hand axes and in the process gain the confidence that comes from making a tool. This process demonstrates how we can have adventure in a variety of ways: designing, working with the hands, and working with the mind as we carry the concept of democratic things further.

Another value this experience has had for me is the breaking of mental and social barriers, which we need to be able to do if we are to solve our problems and create a decent society that works for *all* people.

At times the outlook appears very dark. It would seem our problems are insurmountable. As with this little hand axe, I was quite sure that I would never make my own. And yet, without consciously focusing on the problem directly, unconscious forces were at work and discovered a solution. This gives me hope that if we can continue searching and caring and supporting one another—we may be able to find the solution to even our worst problems.

P.S. The broad hatchet from Shikoku finally arrived. It is a veritable gem. Actually, two came—a left- and a right-handed one—polished to a mirror finish and gently wrapped in small white towels.

W. Coperthwaite

To Make an Axe:

1. Trace the pattern on the next page on annealed (temperable) steel, $5/16$-thick.

2. Cut out the axe head with a hacksaw.

3. Smooth all edges with a file, and file the bevel to make the cutting edge. (For a right-hander, the bevel should be on the right, for a lefty on the left.)

4. Drill two rivet holes.

5. The face should be slightly hollowed, like a shallow gouge. To do this, carve a hollow (6 inches long and $1/4$ inch deep) in a chopping block. Heat the axe head until it is glowing red, then hammer it into the hollow with the bevel side up.

6. To harden the steel, heat it to glowing red and plunge it immediately into cold water.

7. To temper the steel, put the axe head in an oven at 475°F for about twenty minutes and allow to cool slowly.

8. Carve a handle of hardwood in the form shown in the photograph and rivet it to the axe head. You can customize the handle's curve and weight to your own preferences.

If one advances confidently in the direction of his dreams, and endeavors to live the life he has imagined, he will meet with a success unexpected in common hours.

—HENRY DAVID THOREAU

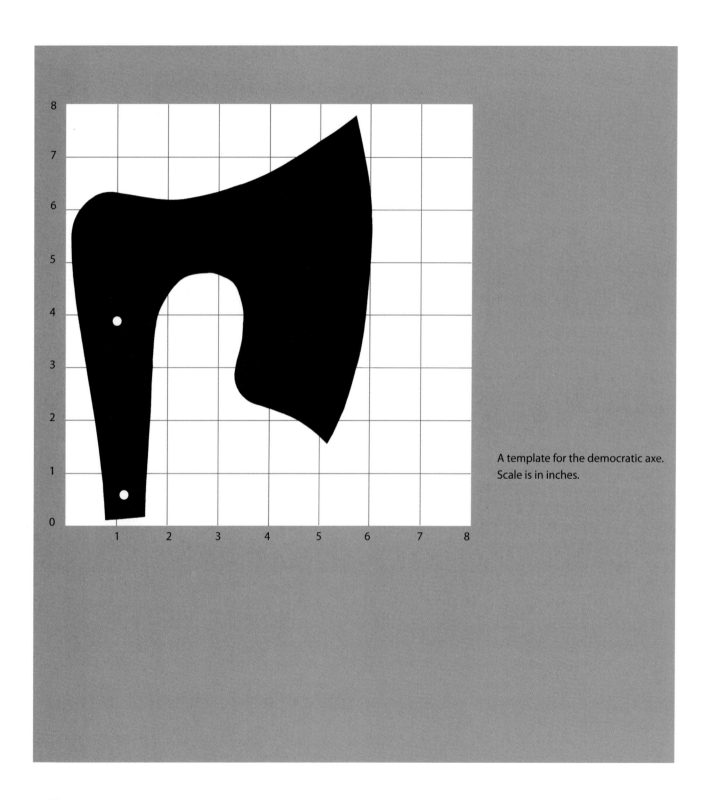

A template for the democratic axe.
Scale is in inches.

Have nothing in your house
that you do not know to be useful
or believe to be beautiful.
            —WILLIAM MORRIS

BEAUTY

THE RHODORA

In May, when sea-winds pierced our solitudes,
I found the fresh Rhodora in the woods,
Spreading its leafless blooms in a damp nook,
To please the desert and the sluggish brook.
The purple petals fallen in the pool
Made the black water with their beauty gay;
Here might the red-bird come his plumes to cool,
And court the flower that cheapens his array.
Rhodora! if the sages ask thee why
This charm is wasted on the earth and sky,
Tell them, dear, that, if eyes were made for seeing,
Then beauty is its own excuse for Being;
Why thou wert there, O rival of the rose!
I never thought to ask; I never knew;
But in my simple ignorance suppose
The self-same power that brought me there,
  brought you.

—Ralph Waldo Emerson

W. Coperthwaite

"Beauty" is one of the most powerful words in our language. The poet John Keats is remembered for equating beauty and truth, and Gandhi for equating truth, god, and love. In this equation, our experiences of beauty, truth, love, and god are facets of one another.

In our society, beauty tends to be visual—a surface, the decoration and ornamentation. We may consider beautiful the picture on the wall, the fancy dishes on the table, the clothes for frolics, the frosting on the cake. Yet increasing numbers of people are now looking at the cake beneath, seeking more substance, and others are dispensing with both frosting and cake and choosing instead the beauty of a whole-grain loaf.

Most of the time, for most of our days, we are confronted with ugliness rather than beauty. But we cannot afford to have our visual sense blighted by the continuous parade of drabness and sham, the cheap and the tawdry. For emotional and physical well-being, we need to be surrounded as much as possible with beauty. If we had this as the goal of our society, we could turn the world into a paradise that would be beautiful to both the eye and the mind.

Surroundings are important. Remember, the dishes and clothes we use for every day are more important to our visual sense and well-being than those used only for special occasions. What matters most is not expense but awareness.

And what is beautiful is easier to live with and care for. If we had fewer things and more meaningful ones, our homes and towns would be less cluttered, less ugly, and more peaceful. Our surroundings have a direct relationship to how tired we get and how happy *we feel*.

Have you ridden in a New York cab lately? Driven into Chicago from the south? Waited for a bus in the Los Angeles airport? Watched the evening news? We can do better.

Many things that appear attractive at first
become ugly to us when we gain deeper knowledge:
a building that took an oppressed class to build,
a tool that will not hold an edge, clothes that shrink
or fade on washing. Are these beautiful?
The way we answer this question has momentous
import for our concept of society.

ORDINARY BEAUTY

There is much beauty that goes unrecognized. With a heightened awareness, we can see beauty where only plainness seemed to exist before.

Have you ever looked closely at a piece of glass? Glass is so common in our culture as to be taken for granted, and yet to our ancestors a few short centuries ago, it was precious. Think of the folk wisdom expressed in a piece of glass. Think, too, of what life would be like if there were no glass for your windows, your bottles, your lenses.

As I write I'm looking up at the sky through a five-foot circle of tempered glass, so clear that it is invisible. What fantastic developments in the realm of glass, from the time when people first found a way to melt sand to these wondrously clear panes of today. Glass does not need to be expensively etched or ornamented to be beautiful. Like so much that surrounds us, glass needs no adornment.

Because something is common, why should we view it as any less wonderful? So much of beauty is in the mind.

The marketplace peddles the current concept of beauty, which is constantly manipulated to create more profits. But those who learn to see beyond this device can be free. If we encourage our own sense of beauty to develop rather than follow the market and fashion, we can live both beautifully and simply.

A factory can produce mittens of equal warmth to those made at home, and at a fraction of the cost. But

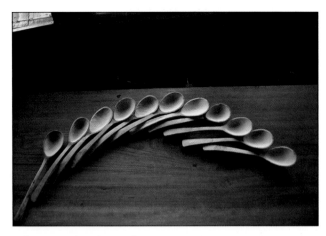

Utilitarian art: hand-carved spoons.

there are other factors that combine to distinguish the home-knit ones from the store-bought.

When we produce an article of clothing for others with concern for their welfare, we knit this concern into the garment. Those who recognize that extra quality will feel a greater sense of care and affection—as well as warmth—when they wear the gift. For those who know this, the hand-knit mittens are more beautiful. Our sense of the beautiful is greatly influenced by knowledge.

While we are often accustomed to think of beauty as visual, once we have looked beneath the surface, we never see quite the same way again. Imagine a newly made boat with its lovely lines, the oiled wood gleaming, the boat of your dreams. Then you discover that it was made of weak, poorly selected wood that will rot quickly and fail suddenly at sea. Is this still a beautiful boat in your eyes? It has the same lines as before, but can we call it beautiful?

We are led to believe that the Egyptian pyramids are an ingenious tribute to human greatness and that as such they are beautiful. But as we grow older we learn that the

---

pyramids are monuments of tyranny and oppression—that slaves in vast numbers died in building these tombs for theocratic rulers, that they are tributes to human inhumanity. Can they ever appear anything but ugly in caring eyes again?

ORNAMENTATION: EXTRANEOUS IS UGLY

Ornament has usurped the place of beauty. Decoration can be fine, so long as it does not interfere with the primary purpose. A spoon is a tool—primarily to eat with, to stir or ladle with. The ornamental corners on the handles of fancy antique silverware interfere with their use. As old and as lovely as they are in certain ways, these sharp corners detract from the utensils' beauty, and I filed mine off.

There are many unnecessary things in our daily lives that take up the largest part of our visual space. We think we can ignore them or tune them out, but they cannot be ignored because they are all about us and impinge on our senses constantly, unconsciously when not consciously noticed, adding to our mental clutter. If in addition we surround ourselves with "art work," we stretch even thinner our capacity for concentration.

Why not have as few things as possible, and these of the finest quality we can afford, dispensing with the nonessentials?

The chair is *the decoration.*

—PETER DENKO

Thoreau said, "A man is rich in proportion to the things he can afford to let alone." Through selectivity we can come into a more intimate awareness of the spirit or nature of those things we use in daily life. Not that ornament need be forbidden, but let beauty first be inward-looking and essential—such as the lining of a shell, of which the inhabitant is unconscious—and not mere outward garnishing.

The feeling that there is a definite ugliness in superfluous things grows on me year by year. I find an increasing joy in being able to live with one less tool, or chair, or book—and to double the joy by finding someone else who needs what I no longer do.

RARITY

Another restrictive view of beauty that deserves critique is the way many people assign higher value for rarity and scarcity. According to conventional wisdom, the "cost of replacement" is a critical factor. If something perishes quickly or is difficult to replace, it tends to be viewed as precious.

Society has put a premium on those objects that are scarce, therefore diamonds, platinum, and sable are valued highly. But this is a violent concept of beauty, based on the premise that for me to be rich you must be poor. There is no intrinsic reason that a gold necklace is more beautiful than one made of seashells. We must create a concept of beauty that is compatible with happiness—

one that relates not to scarcity but to plenty. We must learn to see beauty in our neighbors living well.

Once, in Mexico, I bought some lovely water glasses. They were extremely cheap and available to almost everyone, at least there. But five thousand miles away from that village marketplace, each one that broke (they didn't take well to sudden immersion in hot water) made me more careful of the rest. Eventually I was treating them as treasures, rarely used and nervously washed.

I came to realize that part of the beauty of a water glass, in addition to being pleasing to the touch of the eye, hand, and lip, was to be pleasing to the touch of the mind as well. Moreover, being easily available, cheap enough for all to afford, and easy to clean and store are also facets of beauty.

In the Mind's Eye

The idea that our sense of beauty is conditioned by experience may seem strange at first blush. But if we agree that knowledge affects beauty, then doesn't it appear reasonable that as we observe, think, and learn, our concept of beauty will change as we grow?

We *can* modify our concept of beauty. Actually, if we do not modify it to be in harmony with our philosophy of life, other forces will condition it to advance their ends. We ourselves must take responsibility for the change or else be manipulated by advertisers or politicians or religious demagogues.

Formerly I doubted the idea that knowledge could influence taste. Then I read in Adelle Davis that if you wanted to get more iron in your diet and you didn't like blackstrap molasses, add a little bit to your bread or cookies each day and gradually increase the measure until you get the proper amount. You will find, so she said, that you have developed a liking for it.

Well, being from Maine, I couldn't accept this without a trial. I applied the theory to yogurt, which at that time I disliked. A year later it had, reluctantly, become a favorite food. Since then I have found that increasing my knowledge will have a great effect on my feelings about beauty, wealth, architecture, social systems, humor, music, boat design—on everything to which I give my attention.

We can condition our concepts of beauty to reconcile them with what we can respect intellectually, so as not to be in conflict with the best that is in us. True beauty must be as pleasing to the mind as to the eye.

Civilization, in the real sense, consists not in the multiplication of wants but in their deliberate reduction. This alone promotes happiness and contentment—and increases the capacity for service.

—Mahatma Gandhi

The peculiar grace of a Shaker chair is due to the fact that it was made by someone capable of believing that an angel might come and sit on it.

—Edward Andrews

If we are ever to develop a nonviolent society,
we must eliminate violence in our concept of beauty.
A Louis XIV chair and a Shaker chair are not equally
beautiful. One was created by a violent, tyrannical
way of life, the other by a peaceful and cooperative
community that made fair treatment of all people
a basic precept—so that the person making
the Shaker chair and the one using it
received equal respect.

BEYOND APPEARANCES

What are some aspects of beauty that affect our feelings besides outward form?

How was a particular product made? By whom? For what purpose? Under what conditions? At what real cost?

With food we may ask: How was it grown? By whom? On what kind of soil? Did the people who grew it or picked it get a fair price?

A tomato grown by a friend has more appeal than one from the store. There is an undeniable beauty in having sprouts and lettuce grown at home rather than shipped across a continent. If we know that our provisions were grown on healthy soil, they are even more beautiful.

On the other hand if we know that the person who picked our fruits or vegetables was not earning a living wage, they are less appealing.

Two Angels were seen
Sitting on a Shaker chair
Designing a wheelbarrow
So delightfuly simple
That it would enchant
A Shaker

Our understanding of beauty has the potential to affect economics, as well. When we buy a car or anything else, we vote with our wallet, giving our support to the production system that manufactured it. For example, when we look at the total cost to society of buying a car, we may start searching for a vehicle made through a more beautiful method of production. We can easily know the dollar cost of an automobile, but what are the human costs? The social costs? How much will it pollute? What are the conditions under which the car we drive was produced? Do we comprehend what the long hours of assembly-line work do to people? Do we approve of a way of doing business that puts millions in the pocket of the manager annually—as salary, not even including the stock options!—while many of the world's people are ill fed, ill clothed, and ill housed?

Years ago, one of my neighbors told of buying potatoes from a local farmer. When he heard that the price was 1½ cents per pound, instead of rejoicing he said, "But you can't raise them for that!" The farmer allowed as how he couldn't. On learning that the cost of production was 5 cents a pound, my neighbor said, "I will pay you 5 cents a pound. It is not to the advantage of either of us for you to go out of business." This is caring economics. It shows a recognition of the interdependency of our lives.

BEYOND THE MATERIAL

Often physical things come to mind when we think of beauty, but fully as important are beautiful attitudes and atmospheres. For instance, what can add more beauty to a home than friends?

How wonderful if our ornamentation could be knowledge, joy, and kindness—treasures that enrich everyone, unlike the baubles we usually use for decoration.

Indigenous Architecture

There are many exciting aspects of native dwellings around the world, too few of which have found their way into modern buildings. This is our loss. Beauty is limited by neither time nor place. If we wish to have more beautiful structures, we could do worse than look to the world of indigenous housing for models.

Anyone who has explored the world of folk shelter has had to face this question: Why are so many indigenous homes so lovely—*trullo, rondavils*, tipis, adobe houses, the fish houses of Grand Manan—and modern ones so cold, harsh, and rigid? I do not have the answer to that question, but if enough of us can be stimulated to explore this fascinating world, together we will find some answers and achieve lovelier shelter as well.

It is not hard to come up with one beautiful house—either to design one, or find one tucked away somewhere—but unless we unlock the secrets of the beauty of folk architecture, our visual world is apt to continue to be blighted by the mass architecture we see everywhere as we drive the roads and lanes of the land.

Part of the problem is the impersonal character of much architecture, structures designed for someone else, for money, for prestige—self-conscious, ego-inflating designs. Until recently, most houses the world over had no architect involved. No money changed hands. Homes were owner and neighbor built. The design was a traditional form handed down from the past. Changes in design were made on a glacial time scale, and all materials were local.

This ensured, at least, that

– the design was proven to be effective;
– the builders had a deep familiarity with the materials and the skills needed, and
– there was a harmony of building materials from one house to the next in a given region.

When I see the unifying beauty of the roofs of irregular slates in parts of France, Norway, and the Cotswolds, or the Japanese roofs that combine shingles of both slate and wood in alternating rows, I get a lift, a feeling of wonder and ecstasy. And I wonder how *we* could achieve such beauty. I am not asking for copies—we are a different people living in a different time. Reproductions are not the answer. Yet can we not capture the spirit of folk designs and build homes that fit our own times and materials as beautifully as our ancestors did? I think that we can, if enough people will take part in the search.

My work with yurts has been the result of one person's search, a specific example of exploration in this rich field—not as something to copy, but hopefully encouragement to others to explore, and a way of reaching out to make contact with people of like minds.

W. Coperthwaite

Another kind of beauty: A bread so good both to the palate and to health that a diet of bread and water would be a delight.

GRANT BREAD

(for one loaf)

- 1/2   ounce yeast
- 1   teaspoon honey
- 13   ounces water at body temperature
- 1   pound whole-wheat flour

Mix yeast and honey in 1/2 cup of the warm water, then let sit to froth for ten minutes. Pour the yeasty mix into the flour and add the remaining water. Mix by hand for several minutes, working from the sides of the bowl to the middle, until the dough feels elastic and leaves the sides of the bowl clean. Put the dough in a tin, covered with a damp cloth, and place it in a warm place for twenty minutes or so, allowing the dough to rise by about a third or until it is an inch from the top of the tin. Bake the bread in the tin at 450°F for 35–40 minutes.

—Doris Grant

Here's a yardstick: That which deprives another cannot be beautiful.

Nonviolent beauty—beauty contained in nonmaterial things, such as a way of life, learning, relationships with others—cannot be stolen and is unlikely to produce envy. These forms of beauty are among those unusual riches that impoverish no one, that can be given away and make everyone richer.

Respect for All Things

Another facet of beautiful living will be an "intimate, personal, kinship relationship" with nature—knowing and being known by nature. Life should be a search for harmony—not a battle, not a challenge—neither dominating nor contending with nature but seeking harmony.

Not only is a more personal relationship with nature desirable but so is a more personal relationship to the world of things, from food to clothes to rocks in the garden wall. We need to surround ourselves with things made with care and affection.

One of our pressing needs is to build a more personal sense of our world. The role that emotional security plays in developing a happy, productive, and concerned person cannot be overstated. If we desire to eliminate prejudice, there is no better place to start than to create personal, meaningful relationships with our surroundings.

For example, washing dishes is a chore for many. There are too many of them, and all too often they have no personal meaning. But when the dishes we use are few, made by ourselves or our friends, or personally sought for their beauty and chosen because they are strong and easily cleaned, each as perfect an example of its kind as we can find, then the experience of dishwashing has been known to change its nature.

Maggie

Dillingham is a small place on Alaska's Bristol Bay. Christmas was two days off, and we were snow bound. The village of Togiak was my destination with the Traveling Museum of Eskimo Culture that I had assembled. Four of us sat in the small airport waiting room hoping the weather would break to allow us to go to Togiak for Christmas. We were thus tied to the airport rather than free to seek out friends in Dillingham.

One of the four was Maggie, a seven-year-old Eskimo. She had been to Anchorage to have a broken arm set and was hoping to be home for Christmas.

I had books to read, letters to write, and craft work to do. As the hours crept by, I began to feel concern for this little girl, traveling alone with nothing to play with.

Now, Maggie was an extremely shy little seven-year-old. A direct approach was definitely out. I settled on making a doll for her first Christmas away from home. The afternoon of Christmas Eve, I managed to scrounge a sock, some buttons, and a bit of stuffing. In my kit were thread, needles, and scissors.

I pretended to completely ignore Maggie, but after an hour her curiosity won out and she was in the seat beside me. After a while, I asked her to thread a needle, then to hold on to the doll while I sewed on buttons for eyes. Eventually we sewed and snipped out a rag doll and made clothes for her. By now we were on a first name basis, and I knew she was in the second grade in Togiak.

For Christmas, Maggie had a doll. We were now good friends. The next day we flew into Togiak. Later that week, when I entered Maggie's second-grade classroom, she burst from her seat, rushed up, and hugged me—broken wing and all. Here was one of life's highlights.

D. Porter

It may be Wilderness without—
Far feet of failing Men
But Holiday excludes the night—
And it is Bells—within.

—Emily Dickinson

Eating at Pete's

During my first few days in the Eskimo village of Hooper Bay, and wanting to learn more about kayak building, I sought out Pete, one of the last two kayak builders there. He was a pleasant, cheerful man of fifty, who spoke a broken English with little confidence. I found him lashing a sled, and after watching him awhile, slowly began taking part by handing him the needed tool or holding a lashing to make it more secure.

We chatted in short "pidjin" phrases interlaced by his comment, "My daughter—she come home soon. We talk good." We had an enjoyable hour of this back and forth until his daughter, a girl of fifteen, did indeed come home, as did his handsome seventeen-year-old son. Both were as fashionably dressed as high school students in any conservative community of the United States—in great contrast to the father, whose clothes were ragged and not suffering from an excess of washing. The children were shy with me, although this stranger was obviously enjoying working with their father.

We all went inside the patchwork house made of scrap wood of every description, gleaned over a quarter of a century from the beaches as well as old packing crates and school debris. On the floor lay a partially skinned seal, which the boy had shot that morning before school, the first catch of the season.

At first glance the place was a wreck—a shambles, with all the possessions of the family in view in one corner or another, or draped over a bunk or beam. Equipment and clothing lay about in various stages of repair or disrepair. Badly torn, greatly worn blankets and quilts were in disarray on the beds.

Seated on the floor, which served alternately as a workshop, butchery, washroom, and play space for the babies, sat the mother—a voluminous woman in a voluminous granny dress—with a face of joy and contentment, cooking seal meat in a battered dishpan over a much-used Primus stove. She spoke no English but made me welcome with the most beautiful of smiles. The son and daughter shrank visibly with an apparent mixture of disbelief and shame—disbelief that a white man had actually crossed their threshold (in a village where this was seemingly unheard of) and shame at the wreckage they called home, knowing from seeing the teacher's house what my world must be like.

The clincher was that the girl and boy became tongue-tied and could not (or would not) translate for their parents. It was not difficult to see the way this was shaping up in their minds, so I started a campaign to win over two teenaged Eskimo friends.

After praising the size of the seal and the boy for having shot it, I ran my eyes across those examples of folk art that are universally present in such houses, tucked in among the wreckage: a kayak stem here, a knife there, a lovely fishhook dangling from a beam, the intricate sewing on a worn-out skin mukluk. The father and I talked, my questions revealing knowledge of their culture and respect for it, so stated as to arouse the curiosity of the children while letting them know that I was a friend and could see beyond torn blankets and a blood-soaked floor to the beauties of the Eskimo way of life. My respect was underscored with Eskimo and Lapp artifacts, which appeared from my shoulder bag. Looking at these drew us together in a close circle. Soon the son was volunteering to locate a certain kind of fishhook, which I had hoped would be there, and the daughter was volunteering words when we got stuck. Through all of this, the mother sat quietly working, with a blissful expression.

After an hour, the room had settled into a relaxed atmosphere—a sharing of artifacts, craft insights, and hunting stories. Then approached a traumatic crossroads. In every home, in every culture, there is a moment of limbo when it is either time to leave or time to be asked to eat. Often it is clear, indisputably clear, that the time has come to exit. At that moment, the father said a few low words in Eskimo, almost a whisper. The children responded in Eskimo with a very firm reply, again almost a whisper. Then, with a sound that seemed to convey, "Damn it, this is my house, I will ask him!" Pete turned to me and said, "You like eat seal meat?" This was almost too much for the children. Their ways had been rejected so many times that they didn't want to hear another *gussuk* (white man) give

excuses for not eating their food. I'm sure I glowed visibly when I responded with, "Yes, I like eat seal meat."

First the rich broth was ladled into battered tin plates, a blessing was said, oddments of tableware were handed out, and we began eating. It was an unexciting dish, until Pete handed me the salt and what had tasted dull turned into an epicure's delight. Slowly the children joined in and we were soon a relaxed family at dinner with an unexpected but welcome guest at the table.

That which is not a necessity is an encumbrance.

—NOMAD SAYING

Eskimo fishhooks.

D. Porter

D. Porter

D. Porter

Have you ever had the experience of apologizing to an inanimate object? When we drop a cup and break it, we violate its nature. All things, be they living or inanimate, have their own nature, spirit, or essence. Whenever we come into contact with anything, we either promote or hinder that essential nature. Unless we seek to understand the nature of the things that surround us, we will be a hindrance rather than a help to our world.

Developing sensitivity and awareness by searching for the basic nature of things is the road to understanding.

When we drop and break a cup, we do violence to its spirit, its purpose, and to the work of the artisan who shaped it. We owe the cup an apology.

Whether running a canoe aground, dulling a chisel on a nail, or puncturing a tire—instead of cursing, we owe an apology. You may respond that the object has no feelings. I would tend to agree with you. But apologies are both given and received, and the effect on the giver may be more important than the effect on the recipient.

When you work you are a flute
through whose heart the whispering
of the hours turns to music.
To love life through labor is to be intimate
with life's inmost secret.
All work is empty save when there is love,
for work is love made visible.

—KAHLIL GIBRAN

WORK / BREAD LABOR

Work, to some, suggests drudgery—prostitution in order to earn a living—something one must do. For others of us, this is a gross misuse of the term: we believe that work is the productive and creative activity that makes human life possible. When the necessary work of the world is shared by all of its people, there need be no painful toil.

The term "bread labor" was coined in the past century by Bondaref and brought to prominence by Tolstoy and Gandhi. It refers to the basic work that is necessary for subsistence. Bread is a symbol and stands for more than the activity of baking bread. Bread labor means all needed work, whether food raising and preparation, the making of clothing and shelter, or caring for children.

Work is one of our most useful learning tools; children love to imitate adults at work. It is drudgery that needs eliminating, not work.

And though examples are extremely important to children as they grow, at this time few children in this culture grow up seeing people do work that they enjoy. We do them a great disservice when we

— work where they cannot see us (at the office or the shop),
— do work that we neither enjoy nor believe in, and
— talk of work as something to avoid.

Work is an interesting and tremendously exciting learning tool when undertaken voluntarily and in ways that do not cripple the spirit.

SEEKING GOOD WORK

I was privileged to grow up among people who enjoyed working with their hands, their minds, and their bodies. There were not many of these people, but there were enough so that as a young person I could see that it wasn't all one way in the world.

During college I wrestled with the problem of what constituted valid life work. I wanted no part in the common prostitution whereby muscle, brains, or talent are sold for the wherewithal to pursue personal goals in spare time.

There were three people in particular who I admired for their sensitivity, their intellectual acuity, their work with their hands, and their dedication to a better society:

— Morris Mitchell, who as president of the Putney Graduate School of Education blended cabinet-

The trail that leads 1½ miles from the road-head to my house can be kept up by one person, but with other matters demanding attention, that job often gets only a lick and a promise instead of a good day's cutting and trimming. It is always a delight to meet someone who appreciates the work necessary to keep a trail open in the Maine woods and is willing to lend a hand. Spending a couple of hours together clearing trail is a pleasant, relaxing catalyst for communication.

making and gardening with his leadership of the school.

— Walter Clark, cofounder of the North Country School in Lake Placid, N.Y., who was equally at home in the classroom, workshop, garden, or sugar bush;

— Scott Nearing, who at ninety-nine was still splitting his own firewood and who had blended writing and lecturing with gardening and building over a long and full life.

I met these men during and after graduate school, and I wish that their examples had come earlier in my life. All three exemplified responsible adult living, showing that work could be enjoyable and also demonstrating that the great pioneering ahead of us lies in the search for a better way of life.

The ideal work will develop and utilize—rather than fragment—the whole person. The work I was seeking needed to

— be physically and intellectually challenging,
— encourage creative thinking,
— advance the cause of a better world, and
— provide for basic needs.

Alas, I was not overwhelmed with offers for employment. And yet approaching a career by way of these principles enabled me to examine various occupations, which made the search more interesting. One of the greatest values of this experience was in finding how little present society asks one to be a complete person and how much fragmentation, frustration, and prostitution are considered normal. But along the way I had the good fortune to stumble on this handful of people who had achieved the personal integration of life that I sought. They became some of my closest friends and staunchest supporters in developing a theory of social design.

After growing up in a world where the norm is to sell a piece of oneself, it is difficult to imagine another way of living. Examples are of tremendous value. Where can one look to see work and play united? Where people disdain retirement? Where vacation, recreation, and hobby are ugly words made necessary by a social disease—forced work. Robert Frost crystallized this thought in his poem *Two Tramps in Mudtime:*

But yield who will to their separation
My object in living is to unite
My avocation and my vocation
As my two eyes make one in sight.

Can there be any greater reproach than idle learning? Learn to split wood at least. . . . Steady labor with the hands, which engrosses the attention also, is unquestionably the best method of removing palaver and sentimentality out of one's style, both of speaking and writing. The scholar may be sure that he writes the tougher truth for the calluses on his palms.

—Henry David Thoreau

The earth's green cover with the few inches of soil which holds the rain and makes plant growth possible is the most important factor in our ultimate survival.

—Walter Clark

Where we find buildings that are ugly, furniture that is ill made, doors that do not close properly, vines and fruit trees clumsily pruned . . . the lack of skill and care which these things represent might simply be the fruit of a wrong attitude toward work itself.

—Thomas Merton

An example of that blending of the intellectual and the physical were the Swiss brothers, scientists Jean and Auguste Piccard, in the early twentieth century. As students they lacked time to do all the assigned reading, because they had to work to earn their way. So they took turns, one reading aloud while the other sawed wood. Thus they each got in a whole day of study and a half a day of labor in a single day—as well as keeping warm.

For confidence and well-being, it is important to feel needed and useful. This is true for people of all ages. In our society, it is mostly the young and the old that are neglected. In our fear of "overworking" them—or by supposing that not needing to work is an advantageous position—we've gone from exploiting children as labor in the mills and mines to allowing them no work, and from sending the aged to workhouses to banishing them to retirement homes. In the process, we are ignoring the wishes and needs of those involved.

Work is one of the primary means whereby a child learns, grows, feels a sense of belonging, and discovers ways of being a useful member of society. For the older person, having work that fits one's nature and capacity gives a sense of purpose and engagement that is extremely important in declining years.

If we have not been helped to see how our life can be useful to the world beyond ourselves, we fail to harvest the full return on our labor.

A Necessary Evil?

Work is so often misunderstood. The prevalent attitude toward hard work is that it is a "necessary evil" and that, while perhaps its burdens ought to be shared—done out of duty—work is definitely not an experience to be enjoyed. Many people learn to accomplish obligatory tasks well, at least efficiently; they dutifully do their share of labor to meet personal or family needs. Yet they consider bread labor less important than art, thought, research, or "creative" activities.

I protest. Bread labor is a primary activity of life, equal to or above these other pursuits in importance.

What if we have been on the wrong track? What if work, including the meeting of mundane needs, were to be recognized as an essential tool in understanding ourselves and our world? What if we were to see that creativity, to be valuable and not merely dilettante, must be rooted in work?

Without labor, our way of life would not exist.

Fair Shares

There is always a basic amount of primary work to be done. The morality behind the concept of bread labor is that when work is spread out evenly among the whole populace no one need suffer from overwork, and all have the benefits of feeling that they are doing their share to make society function. Some cannot work, of course: they are too old, too young, or too sick. This is natural. These people are dependents. But what able-bodied person wishes to think of him- or herself as dependent, parasitic, incapable of carrying a fair share of the load?

Gandhi incorporated bread labor into his daily life as a basic element. He would willingly choose to do the most avoided tasks, those assigned to the lowest class, for instance, sweeping dung from the streets and emptying the privies. He felt that if we want to have a classless society where all are equal, then the freest, the wealthiest, the strongest, the wisest, and the most respected should voluntarily take up the most despised work. This would help to remove class prejudice and raise work to being celebrated instead of despised.

Somehow we must find a way to develop a society of people who refuse to live at the expense of others, be they nearby or on the far side of the globe.

Voluntary Slavery?

We all agree that slavery—the selling of people—is wrong. Isn't it equally wrong to sell oneself? Employers make it so easy: pleasant working space, interesting companions, large salary, pension and insurance plans, short hours, long holidays, stock options, bonuses, opportunities for advancement, and Muzak to boot. But if this is not work that you feel good about doing—work that you do only for the pay and the benefits—it remains prostitution.

Many people believe that they must tolerate their existing level of self-exploitation into the future. But if we look at our lives honestly, we may speed the time when such self-exploitation is no longer necessary. If we can reduce the amount we sell ourselves a little more each month, each year we can come closer to the time when rather than

Great thoughts hallow any labor. Today I earned seventy-five cents heaving manure out of a pen, and made a good bargain of it. If the ditcher muses the while how he may live uprightly, the ditching spade and the turf knife may be engraved on the coat-of-arms of his posterity.

—Henry David Thoreau

And if you cannot work with love but only with distaste, it is better that you leave your work and sit at the gate of the temple and take alms of those who work with joy.

For if you bake bread with indifference, you bake a bitter bread that feeds but half man's hunger. And if you sing though as angels, and love not the singing, you muffle man's ears to the voices of the day and the voices of the night.

—Kahlil Gibran

selling ourselves 100 percent of the working day it will be only 70 percent, or 50 percent, or 30 percent.

Such improvements will be of momentous importance to the individual and to society. The first step is to recognize the extent to which we prostitute ourselves.

The common practice of being miserable in a job creates a dangerous atmosphere, which can affect growing children who see the adults they love relating negatively to their work, coming home frustrated and unhappy. Imagine being able to face your kids honestly, having them know you cannot be bought—that you are among those who do not have a price. It is so much healthier for a child to see parents recognizing that their way of living is wrong and seeking a remedy rather than continuing to rationalize unhappiness, thereby encouraging the child to follow the same pattern.

Even short of quitting an ill-fitting job and finding a new one, there are ways in which improvements can be made. Try to find possibilities for growing and learning in your present work. Concentrate on those aspects of the job in which you most fully believe. Try to reduce the time you spend in ways that seem counterproductive, unethical, or wasteful, and apply the saved hours to work that you enjoy and feel is worthwhile.

If we could all sell ourselves as little as possible, this would have a very positive effect on the society around us.

In fact, we can have a shorter workday anytime we choose. We need only to decide to live with less "goods." Going without the Coke, tobacco, and alcohol is easy, and so too junk foods, coffee, and tea. Also, by taking care of our clothes we can make them last longer, freeing ourselves from the fashion scam, and likewise with our cars and equipment.

One of many reasons for living simply is that instead of earning money to buy superfluities we work to provide for primary needs, which means fewer hours total need to be spent in hired employment.

If all able-bodied people in our society would contribute their share of effort, the hours required of everyone would be reduced dramatically, and the necessity of selling oneself would be greatly reduced. When we consider as well the desire of many to do more of their own home-centered labor—building a house, growing food, doing mechanical maintenance and repairs, sewing—this further reduces the number of hours people are obligated to contribute to a collective labor pool.

Scott Nearing reasoned that if every able-bodied adult would contribute four hours a day of bread labor, the world's work could get done. Four hours seemed to him a generous amount of time. Gandhi thought that two hours a day would be enough to supply all basic needs. Modern tools have increased productivity considerably since these estimates were made.

If the world's necessary labor were distributed fairly, work could become a beautiful and exciting part of life. Happiness further lessens the effort needed to do any job. Baking bread, for example, under the right conditions can be a joyful experience, but under pressure of too much work, too low a return, in alien conditions, and using ingredients of questionable quality, baking is drudgery.

Borderline Economics: A Tarahumara Ball

The Tarahumara Indians live in northern Mexico, in the state of Chihuahua, in an enormous canyon the size of the Grand Canyon called Barranca de Cobre. Known as "the running Indians," they make a game of kicking a wooden ball (the size of a baseball) over a 20-mile course—barefoot.

A friend returned from visiting the Tarahumara with a new specimen of one of their hand-carved balls. He had paid the paltry price of half a U.S. dollar asked for it. My first reaction was one of sadness for an economic system that allows such exploitation. I had no clear idea of the exchange rate of pesos for dollars and no idea what an American dollar could buy in that region. And I did not know how long it took to carve such a ball.

I started asking friends for their thoughts about the time it would take to carve a wooden ball like this, starting with a 3-inch diameter aspen limb, 3 inches long.

Opinions ranged from two days to my estimate of two hours. The results exceeded the most optimistic guess: my first ball of white cedar took twenty minutes. I was both amazed and pleased at the short time needed. A skilled native carver would certainly shorten that time.

The economics of ball carving for the Tarahumara now looked quite different. Though still exploitation, the sale was more equitable than I'd earlier assumed. I'm almost tempted to head for Barranca de Cobre to make a few balls myself—"now and then, rainy days."

To Make a Ball:

Step 1. Make a 3-inch-diameter cylinder of clear softwood (white pine, aspen, white cedar), 3 inches long.

Step 2. Mark cylinder.

Step 3. Whittle away the top and bottom of the cylinder, rounding the edges.

Step 4. Mark the block, as in drawing.

Step 5. Cut away the new corners.

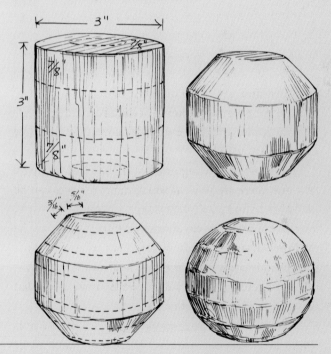

You come away from the great factory saddened, as if the chief end of man were to make pails; but in the case of the country man who makes a few pails now and then, rainy days, the relative importance of human life and of pails is preserved, and you come away thinking of the simple and helpful life of the man—and would fain go to making pails yourself.

—Henry David Thoreau

Karmakai's Carved Bowls

We were in Altai, that mountainous region where China, Mongolia, Kazakhstan, and Siberia meet. The Soviet Union had recently come unglued, and we could move freely in Siberia for the first time in my lifetime. We rode the Trans-Siberian Railway and took side trips by bus, jeep, and truck. We were on a trip of exploration to search out which among the old craft techniques had survived the Soviet era. As a thread to tie the expedition together, we were seeking out people who used crooked knives or who worked birch bark.

Someone sent us to see Karmakai, a small, cheerful Kazak man in his eighties. His face and hands were a lovely, deeply wrinkled russet—a man who had spent his life in the sun and wind. He was happy to show us how he carved bowls.

Immediately after finding out the purpose of our visit, he split a pine log in half and sawed a piece to length. Then, with his hand axe, he alternately chopped and shaved the outside of the bowl. Next, using his small homemade adz he hollowed out most of the interior and then began smoothing the inner curve with his crooked knife.

By this time, sweat was rolling down his gnarled face. He was working hard, unused to demonstrating his skills, and we were the first Americans he had met as well. The result of his effort was a lovely bowl whose shape was reminiscent of the tea bowls of Tibet and Nepal. The ones with which I was familiar were neatly turned on a lathe,

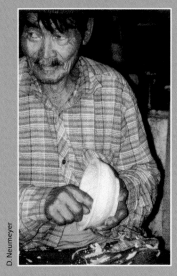

D. Neumeyer

often of a beautiful wood such as apricot or walnut, and lined with silver.

I assumed that Karmakai's carved bowls were a fluke, an exception to the rule of lathe-turned bowls. It was delightful to see the freer beauty of his bowls in comparison to the precision of the production ones. I thought that he worked in this way because he didn't have a lathe. Less than a week later, I was surprised to see the same free, hand-carved form in a large bowl, 18 inches in diameter, in a small village museum. This bowl was very old, with signs of much use.

The next wedge to separate me from my preconceptions was in another museum, a bowl similar in style to Karmakai's, but small and shallow, the same form expressed in a richly different way.

This design and way of carving could no longer be seen as an aberration, the unique creation of one person. Here was a design specific to these Kazak people and their nomad ancestors. Because the basic form of the lathe-turned bowls and the hand-carved bowls are so similar, I assume they stem from a common ancestry. I suspect the hand-carved technique predates the turned version—that it was a style developed by nomads who carried few tools with them, and who made an occasional bowl for family or friends as needed.

Eventually demand grew and was met by sedentary craftsmen in towns who started to mass produce bowls on their lathes for sale.

A New World of Work

Imagine if instead of being so preoccupied with our "hourly wage" we were all to set aside a piece of time each day to contribute to the world's labor pool. Imagine a world in which nobody is for hire—where nobody works for pay, nearly all work being done for the enjoyment, for the feeling of being useful, or for the desire to learn. Everyone would be required to do his or her own work, or else convince others to trade labor.

Doctors would sweep their own floors; bankers would wash their own windows. The CEO of General Motors would change his own oil. Princes? They wouldn't exist outside of storybooks. Inherited position has no place in any decent society I can imagine.

The challenge would be using those resources in the most efficient way to produce necessities we cannot make (or prefer not to make) at home—dental instruments, jet airplanes, oil refineries, steel mills, and so on. I believe these things could be supplied with between one and two hours per day from each of us. Many jobs that are dreadful when done for long hours are actually interesting and enjoyable when done on a briefer schedule.

The reasoning in support of a system requiring one hour per day of organized, efficient production at bread labor is based on three premises:

1. That *all* able-bodied people work—no exceptions. This means that bankers and brokers, presidents and professors all do their stint.

2. That this is not all the bread labor needed, but only the organized, scheduled time that is required of all. You will contribute other bread labor at your own pace when you cultivate your garden, knit your socks, or build your home.

3. When we are working only a few hours at a stretch our production per hour will be much higher than normal, thus reducing the number of hours needed overall.

If we discovered that 400 hours per year would suffice to meet all our basic needs, there would be two good consequences:

1. The labor pool would be increased greatly by the addition of former dependents who would now be able to take their place and do their share of the work. Children would be able take part much earlier. Would this be exploitation? No! The trouble with child labor in the early

---

Those who live without working are either beggars or thieves.

—Proudhon

No order of society can last in which one man says to another, "You work and toil, and earn bread, and I will eat it."

—Abraham Lincoln

I belong to a church where there are neither harmoniums nor pews, but this law: Only those belong who work for a living.

—Pierre Ceresole

days of industrialization was the misuse of children—overwork, inhumane conditions, poor food, and danger (physical, moral, spiritual). In revulsion, society overreacted with stringent child labor laws. Work is a primary tool for growth and now children are denied this opportunity for learning. If the world's work could be accomplished by one to two hours per day per person, we would be less shocked at the idea of children being asked to do the work of their choice.

2. If we have 400 hours to contribute to society yearly, we might choose to work 40 hours per week for ten weeks and thereby have our service completed for that year, or we might prefer to work four hours per day for one quarter of the year. Many would be interested in working at different tasks each year. For example, I would enjoy spending ten weeks in a shoe factory one year, working in a print shop another, packing fish another, or harvesting seaweed, driving a truck, working on an auto assembly line, driving a snowplow, being a fire lookout. None of these jobs is so demanding of skill that a person cannot succeed as a laborer in a ten-week stint. Jobs requiring more skill would require more stability. This could be balanced with a credit system, with the less desirable jobs gaining higher credit.

In my vision of this transformed world of work, there is no need to be fixed in location as we do our year's worth of labor. One year I might be on a Finnish farm, another in a Korean pottery studio, another taking part in a forestry project in Malaysia. The possibilities are limitless, if we design ways to make the new arrangements work.

Some will worry that this system has too many people and too little pay, but if the pay were to remain constant as the hours decrease, who would complain? Why should unemployment be a problem in an economy with enough goods? We need only shorten the hours and share the work and the goods to solve the problem of excess labor.

> If no one would work for another, what would be
> the effect—morally, economically, and socially?
> Once we move in the direction of neither bossing
> nor being bossed, we either take a big loss in income
> or we find in ourselves a growing commitment
> to simplicity, self-reliance, knowledge, and skill;
> to the extent that something is simple and easy
> to make, it becomes easier to have
> and therefore more available.

No More Bosses

Commonly workers are divided into bosses and those being bossed (often both roles are played by the same person, for each boss in turn has a boss). I'm suggesting a society in which no one is permanently in a position of authority. Direction and supervision are necessary in many activities, but this does not mean that these functions need always to be performed by the same people.

When we realize that we have as great a need for fully developed people as we do for efficient factory production, we will be more ready to transform the work roles as necessary for efficient functioning and optimal human development. An exciting byproduct would be a happier, more developed citizenry, which would also be more productive, with less malingering and less sabotage. Genuine sharing of authority and direction increases respect for the work and for the person in charge.

Buckminster Fuller made the often misunderstood statement that "no one should work for a living." By that did he mean that no one should work? No! Work most certainly will continue to be done, but not by coercion and bribery. One should work for the love of it, the joy of it, the excitement of it—to be of service—to be of use—to learn. Why must there be such a close relationship between work and income? Imagine if people would work for satisfaction and not merely for pay. And if no one would work for another for hire, or no one would do certain tasks, many people would have to start taking care of themselves.

If everyone refused to work for those who are wealthy, their money would become useless and they too would have to work for themselves. By this means a class society based entirely on economics would disappear. We usually think of redistribution of wealth as needing to come about by taxation or by militant uprising. Yet imagine social change coming about thanks to an educated, responsible, self-reliant population that refuses to work for the rich—a democratic and nonviolent social revolution. Even Croesus would have to count all that gold himself.

The ultimate power lies with us: we, the people. . . . Only our lack of awareness limits us.. If *we* refuse to buy the pollutants and the junk, *they* would not make them.

Rest is necessary, and a change of pace and activity
is stimulating, relaxing, and productive. Yet I object
to the idea that it is a natural human need to have
hobbies, take vacations, and retire. If we are doing work
that we believe in, that we enjoy, that engages us fully,
we do not need diversions and relief. We can get
the rest we need or a change of pace by shifting
to another facet of our work or by visiting friends
who share our interests and teach us about their own
pursuits. Those who feel "the need to get away"
with vacations and retirement have not had the joy
of finding the right job. Productive leisure is
more satisfying than non-productive leisure.

Recreation—an ugly word
(Right up there with retirement and entertainment)
Suggesting dissatisfaction, boredom,
The need to escape.

What if: we did work that we liked
By choice—that we're good at—
And could shift to other work
When muscles or neurons tired?
What then happens to vacation, holiday, leisure?

Last week I made a chair for a friend.
Was it work?
It was a "vacation" from splitting wood
Which was a "vacation" from writing
Which was a "vacation" from hauling supplies
Which was a "vacation" from work on the chair.

If we do not move swiftly to less
     retiring
               and
          recreating
We may wreck creation.

C. Canney

Caleb's first spoon.

Exhilaration—is within—
There can no Outer Wine
So royally intoxicate
As that diviner brand
The Soul achieves—Herself—

—Emily Dickinson

It is good to build into our lives work that
tires physically—work that is hard enough to make us
welcome the help of others and welcome
a good night's sleep.
If you were to dump good fuel oil regularly,
it would be shocking. You would lose friends rapidly
and possibly end up in court, yet you can squander
energy in jogging and tennis—
or in driving a sport utility vehicle—
and be in style.

PRODUCTIVE VERSUS POINTLESS WORK

Many of us are concerned that so much of the world's
material, time, and energy is spent on space programs,
weaponry, and the military. These are tremendously dangerous aspects of our society, wasteful and insensitive to
human needs. But among those of us who are aware of
this sickness and oppose it, how many note that already
we are spending more on sports than on all the military
programs combined? If one-half our population spends
one and one-half hours each week in sports related activities—playing, watching, and earning money for equipment, tickets, travel costs, and so on, the total expenditure
of money must be greater than our expenditures for
weapons.

In addition to the financial issues, think of the tremendous amounts of energy and time spent on exercising—
drilling and fitness games and sports. What a boon to humanity if these energies could be channeled in ways that
would alleviate suffering, without any loss in the fitness
involved. Wouldn't it be grand instead of jogging to pedal
exercisers that generate and store electricity?

If anyone demanded that we lift weights and set them
down again until exhausted, it would be considered torture, yet in athletic training we do this all the time. Why

Handmade Toys

There is something especially delightful about handmade toys—an elusive quality that comes from care and affection that evades impersonal production.

I've been scouring the world for democratic designs: low in cost, simple to make, yet beautiful to the mind as well as the eye—pleasing to touch and functioning well. The following are some favorite toys that can be made easily by a parent or by an older youngster for a younger.

These foxes came from Kakunodate in northern Japan and can be made by splitting a piece of green wood—a limb or small trunk about 3 inches in diameter by 4 inches long—into eight pieces. With an amazingly small amount of whittling the little foxes hidden in the wood begin to appear.

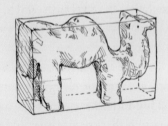

Out of Iraq comes this camel made from a piece of 2 by 6. With a little change here and there, it becomes also a horse, a deer, or a cow.

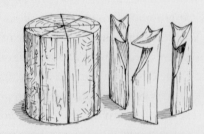

The Siberians make a simple box of birch bark for children called a cricket cage. Seven pieces of bark are needed, one with a hole in it.

Score on the dotted lines, dip in hot water, and fold the edges on the dotted lines. Then pop them together.

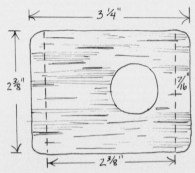

Remember that the inside of the birch bark is the toughest side and should be out. Over time it ages beautifully and looks like leather.

One of my favorites is this reindeer from Finland made from a wooden shingle. When I look at it I see a child begging its father for a toy and this extremely creative man making this ephemeral reindeer in a few minutes.

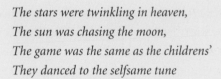

Toys of this sort satisfy doubly, bringing joy to the child and to the maker. If you know of other beautiful toys that are simple to make please write to me about them.

The stars were twinkling in heaven,
The sun was chasing the moon,
The game was the same as the childrens'
They danced to the selfsame tune

—A.E. (GEORGE RUSSELL)

not hook up the weight machines in the gym to produce the energy to light the school? Why not seek a way to build up your body and help others at the same time?

I have not always been opposed to sports. I spent eight years using a long stick to hop over a bar, and I have greatly enjoyed mountain climbing, skiing, and tennis. But the idea of sport as presently conceived has begun to trouble me. I see injustice in my playing while many suffer from war, malnutrition, overwork, poor health, and inadequate shelter and clothing. (There is a long list, and you probably have your own.) I am not asking that we live a joyless life of misery and guilt; I ask only that we become aware of this suffering and design our lives so that we help rather than hinder the world's progress toward equality and justice. That does not mean an austere life with no fun. Pleasure can be found in many ways. With some practice, it can even be found in relieving suffering.

There are also sports and games that do not necessitate a great deal of equipment or need special fields or courts. Sandlot ball with the neighborhood children takes only a ball and bat and a vacant lot—no special shoes or uniforms. Hiking in the mountains does not require the expensive gear sold by the mountaineering houses. Most of the people I know who climb would have no difficulty in giving money to a needy child instead of spending it on a new pair of boots, but it simply does not cross their minds.

You say, "Why not attack television sets instead of climbing boots? Think of all the garden tools represented by the cost of a TV set." You are right, of course. The beer, the TV, and the potato chips are much less necessary and less useful than climbing boots and backpacks, but I'm assuming that the madness of spending life's energy on producing, buying, and watching a TV is obvious to anyone who would be reading this.

I'm very troubled by the amount of vicarious living we do, the time we spend watching someone else play ball or have adventures. The story goes that William Baden-Powell got the idea for the Boy Scouts from seeing a crowd of people watching a soccer match. He suddenly realized that the crowd should have been playing rather than watching.

As a people, we live vicariously much of the time: we watch someone else's drama, ball games, sex life, or adventure, and listen to someone else's music. Instead of vicarious ball games, how about a real game of split wood—or plant garden—or catch a porcupine for supper?

Take a brilliant person working on weapons design at a high salary. This is negative work, no matter how high the quality. You, on the other hand, in making a garden have contributed more toward building a better world, even though that contribution may go unrecognized.

I look ahead to a time when young people will demand useful and necessary work to do. This will not be a result of laws and regulations saying who can and who cannot work, but rather will be a time of recognition by everyone that productive, creative work is a birthright. I see a time when all will recognize our need to feel useful and needed by the society around us—knowing that only through work, lovingly done, will come the growth and sense of belonging that are a part of mature adulthood.

Re-examine all you have been told at school or church
or in any book, dismiss what insults your own soul, and
your very flesh shall be a great poem.

—WALT WHITMAN

EDUCATION / NURTURE

Most of us fall into the error of assuming that going to school and becoming educated are one and the same. Although good schooling and good teaching can be delightful, and can aid greatly in someone's advancement, they are not fundamental to education—*learning* is.

Perhaps "nurture" is a better word to use, as it is less loaded at the present time with misconceptions than "education." How can we best develop a nurturing attitude and a nurturing atmosphere? What are the elements in the environment of a young creature that promote optimal growth—encouraging the learner to thrive, mentally and physically, in skills and in creativity?

Much of my life has been spent in classrooms. As a student, I enjoyed school thoroughly. I was one of the few for whom the system worked, as school was a positive enhancement to my growth. However, such was not the case with many of my classmates. One of the sources of my sadness about those years is the realization of how many failed—failed unnecessarily. This is the shame of our system, a system set up so that for some to succeed others *must* fail: the sacrifice of the many to the few. Along with this comes the subtle but deeply seated lesson (learned by example) that exploitation is laudable and that tyranny is normal. For so many, school was a parade of failures, one after the other, year after year, with ever more "proof" of inadequacy.

As I grew to adulthood, I came to recognize that this treatment of our young is an inexcusable crime with very widespread effects, a failure that more than any other seems to me to be at the core of our social problems.

No programs in medicine, space research, or highway improvement can begin to compare with education in importance, yet we give those other fields much higher priority. Why do we pay more to leaders in auto manufacturing than teachers and child-care providers? Do we really think cars are more important than human enlightenment? We skim off or "high grade" our young and put the best performers into medicine, management, science, and finance. How many excellent personalities capable of working with children have been lost to these professions because of their higher status and pay? If we would pay a million a year for someone to head up an education program, I feel it would be found fully as profitable to society as the manufacturer of cars.

I suggest we do away with the distinction between teacher and student. Ideally we would all be learners, for even if advanced in some areas, we are each woefully ignorant in others. Growing and developing should be lifelong activities—one of the most pleasurable and exciting experiences of life, at all ages.

No one has ever been educated in school or college. The reason is simply that youth itself—immaturity—is an insuperable obstacle to becoming educated. . . . Education comes later, usually much later. The very best thing for our schools to do is to prepare the young for continued learning in later life by giving them the skills of learning and the love of it.

—Mortimer Adler

The Right Atmosphere

One of the most important aids to learning is an atmosphere in which learning is actively and joyfully taking place in the lives of those around us—a situation made remarkable by its rarity in life today.

In selecting what specific material is best for others to learn, be they children or adults, we open ourselves to almost certain error. If, on the other hand, we seek to build a learning atmosphere where the student can choose, we are on firmer footing. If we seek to be the best person we can become—a person eagerly seeking to learn and grow, one willing to share this self, honestly, with those around us—perhaps in this way we can create that atmosphere most conducive to personal growth in those we touch.

Einstein said, "The only rational way to educate is by example—if we can't help it, a warning example." By watching those around us, we do learn. Against any attempt to impose an education, sensitive people will rebel—openly if they can, secretly if they must.

A teacher must want to be with the student, and vice versa, for the process to work. There must be a reason to be together, other than threat, for education to flourish.

The future learning centers envisioned here will not need to test people to see how much they know but will interview them to learn how the center could do a better job. The true test of the program will be the students' (and teachers') freer spirits, greater self-confidence, heightened intellectual curiosity, increased creativity, and wider cultural perspective.

School has become a forced experience, required, with children drafted into it. It would be reasonable for them to ask, "If learning is such a fine thing, why do you have to force it on us?"

Learning and growing are fun—all organisms enjoy the experience, which is the natural state of being. Learning becomes painful only when we disrupt its natural patterns and demand compliance.
Compulsion and education are antithetical.
When the fun and excitement have fled,
we must redesign our learning atmosphere.
We should be able to offer such an exciting world
to students that they will never need threats,
bribes, or stimulants to learn.

A Community of Learners

As a society one of our greatest expenditures of time, effort, and substance is for the schooling of the young. Not only is this an unfair distribution of society's wealth, the effort is not succeeding. Putting such disproportionate emphasis on schools is not the most efficient way to ensure the fullest development of children. The sacrifice of society's energy to this one age group is a tyranny of the young over the old (perpetrated, of course, by the well-intentioned but misguided old). In many homes we have an almost complete ignoring of the elderly.

Grandmother should be as well cared for as the grandchild. In terms of education, the beauty of this more equitable approach is that a well-cared-for, fully developed Granny is a wonderful example to the young of a growing, creative, happy older person.

Schools should be for the use of the community as a whole—learning centers for people of all ages and interests. Perhaps you are thinking that this would detract from the development of the young, but rest assured: if we could create an atmosphere in which learning was exciting and interesting for adults, this would go a long way toward awakening interest in the children.

Children have a need to see healthy, curious, creative

adults in action. Likewise, adult conversation is a precious learning resource for a child.

FOOD

I am troubled by the increasing ingestion by the young of substances either directly harmful to their growth (for instance, drugs, including tea, coffee, and tobacco) or indirectly harmful, preventing their bodies from getting needed nutrition (as with sweets and carbonated beverages). It is difficult to comprehend how we can be so uncaring, insensitive, and ignorant as to allow the temptation of soda machines in the school while professing to have our children's welfare at heart. The Swiss at one time put a tax on white bread, which was used to lower the price of whole-grain loaves in order to encourage sales of the healthier bread. It would be a pleasure to see a community put an added charge on the price of carbonated soft drinks and use this revenue to lower the cost of milk and fruit juices in the school. That would at least get schools out of the ridiculous position of encouraging junk "foods."

If we could design an atmosphere in which learning and personal growth were so much more interesting, exciting, and appealing than TV, pot, junk foods, and crime, those self-destructive diversions would fade into obscurity. Of course, if we had a fully enlightened citizenry, there would be no adults willing to make their living by exploiting children through dealing in harmful products. It is fun to imagine a world in which nobody would be willing to traffic in tobacco and drugs. If some people really wanted them, they would have to grow (as well as roll) their own. No, I'm not so mentally adrift as to believe that such a society will come about soon, but I do believe that if we could discover the keys to education those keys would be doubly beneficial, liberating the purveyor as well as the consumer of the various kinds of junk food and junk media.

Watching the TV screen—which at its best is vicarious learning—is keeping the young from activities that use their minds and bodies more actively and creatively. I fear that we have created for our children a very unreal, dull, and boring world.

LEARNING WHILE WORKING

Out of fear of misusing children, we have deprived them of the opportunity to do real work.

The work of most adults is hidden from the children. Even worse, most of the adults they meet do not enjoy their work.

As a result of this coercion, and the corresponding lack of opportunities for fully applied imaginations, is it any wonder that kids turn for their thrills to stimuli that are antigrowth and antisocial?

Kids need to see productive work being undertaken by those around them and to be given an opportunity to take part at an early age. Useful work as a learning tool has largely been ignored by our educational system. Not only

---

My own idea of an ideal negative action is to get rid of your TV set. It is cheating to get rid of it by selling it or giving it away. You should get rid of it by carefully disassembling it with a heavy, blunt instrument. Would you try to get rid of any other brain disease by selling it or giving it away?

—WENDELL BERRY

Puzzle Adventure

Many people like puzzles. The Eskimos I have met are especially fond of them. Puzzles are easily carried and are a great help in "breaking the ice" in new social situations.

One day in a village on the Bering coast of Alaska, I went to visit an Eskimo kayak maker. He was not at home, so I sat down to wait. His wife was busy making biscuits. There were also three little ones shyly hiding from this strange visitor.

Out with a puzzle—and out came the kids. This is a fine puzzle for trips because all you need is a scissors and about six feet of soft cord or lightweight rope. To set up the puzzle, double the cord and loop it through one of the handles as shown in the drawing. Then take the two loose ends of cord and pass these through the other handle. Tie the ends to your belt or to a doorknob, or have a friend hold them. The challenge is to remove the scissors without using the ends of the cord. (No, you may not cut the cord or unscrew the scissors; this isn't a trick.)

The Eskimo children pondered and juggled and jiggled and pondered, completely absorbed. This was too much for the mother. She came and looked down over the heads of the children for a few moments. Then, dusting the flour from her hands onto her apron, she picked up the scissors and solved the puzzle at once. She was only the third person I had seen do this immediately by inspection. I asked if she had ever seen this puzzle before, and she said no.

Upon returning home the husband saw the puzzle and was eager to try. When it came time for me to leave the village three days later, he was still happily working at it. His wife had not mentioned the fact that she had already solved it.

I learned that puzzle in Scandinavia where I was told it was used in the olden days when scissors were scarce and precious. The women attached their scissors to their belts by a long cord fastened in this way. They were always near at hand, and the children could use them within the length of the cord. When a young girl had learned how to free the scissors she was rewarded with a pair of her own, fastened to her own belt. The status this conveyed ensured that she would never tell the younger ones how to solve the puzzle.

Puzzles are fun in the solving. A demonstration of the solution deprives others of the joy of finding the solution on their own.

Challenge: To get both beads together.

51

do students learn in the doing of the work but also grow in emotional stability as they see the work of their hands being of use to others. For example, while the family is gathering and stacking firewood for winter, encourage children to make stacks of their own. Then, at Christmas time, use only wood from those stacks, letting the children see very directly that their work is keeping the family warm.

In a small French village in the Middle Ages, three young men were wheeling barrows of stone up a ramp. When asked what he was doing, the first replied with some asperity, "Any fool can see that I'm moving stone." The second replied more cordially, "I'm building a wall." The third was heard singing as he approached and replied to the question with a sparkling eye, "I'm building a cathedral." Every youngster should have the opportunity to build their own "cathedral."

Teaching as a Violent Activity

Unless supported by a request or invitation from one who wishes to be helped, teaching is violent. The cow does not force milk on the calf but waits until the calf is ready to suck.

Such a request may be explicit or implied but it must occur, otherwise so-called education will be an invasion—a violation—of privacy, of private mental space.

Most teaching:

— is *presumptuous*, assuming that one person knows what another should know;
— is *ugly*, as is any act that violates another person;
— *clutters the mind* with unabsorbed trivia;
— is *uneconomical, wasteful, and destructive* of our greatest wealth: human potential and creativity;
— is *paternalistic*, developing dependent rather than free and free-thinking people; and
— is *destructive of the teacher's potential* as well as that of the student.

Harold Rugg used to tell a story about sending young teachers out into the educational wilderness to try to improve schools. "Always try to send two," he advised. "Alone it is very difficult to survive as a revolutionary force. People are similar to logs in a fire. One alone cannot continue to burn, but requires at least one other to keep the flames alive. The pioneer teacher needs another sympathetic body to keep the flames of enthusiasm burning. "

Teaching as Collaboration

Teaching is a dangerous occupation, setting the teacher up in the eyes of the society, in the eyes of the students and, I'm afraid, in the teacher's own eyes as one who "knows. "

This is neither healthy nor conducive to a teacher's personal growth. If instead we would make freedom to grow our top priority for ourselves and others, we would be well on the way to building a healthy society.

We have talked too long of sacrifice being laudable, with parents and teachers thinking of themselves as sacrificing their lives to their children. This is an example of good intentions without adequate knowledge causing harm.

Certainly there are times of crisis when it *is* admirable to sacrifice one's self for others, but as a steady diet what we need most is for our parents, teachers, and neighbors to be living examples of healthy, growing people whose searches for sensitivity, awareness, and understanding act as supports and beacons for us. Factual knowledge is relatively easy to learn—*when the desire is present to learn*—but is relatively useless unless tempered by sensitivity, love, and understanding. As Carl Rogers observed, "Only that which is *relatively* unimportant can be taught by one person to another."

Our society has many examples of expert knowledge lacking an ethical base—witness scientific brilliance invested in developing weapons of mass murder, mathematics used to manipulate the market for unearned gain, artistic talent used to deceive the public in advertising. Factual knowledge, unless couched in a mind concerned for the well-being of the social body, will be used against life and health. Learning without tender-heartedness tends to cause harm.

If the main reason a person teaches is for the money, then it is outright prostitution. "Why else would someone teach?" you ask. First should be for the enjoyment. Second might be the role it plays in the building of a better world. Third could be for the personal learning that takes place when teaching is properly done. Some teachers find that preparing and then presenting material in a class with the right atmosphere sharpens their own knowledge and understanding.

I would like to see teaching become a role neither sought nor imposed but assumed only upon invitation from students. (Imagine if political office were attained in similar fashion.) This vision assumes that the role of teacher is fluid: all people may be teachers at various times in their lives, yet more often, and for a greater part of the time, would be students. The mature person in such a society would be someone who is willing to share, upon request, what has been learned. This would increase immensely the number of people available for guidance and teaching with corresponding improvement in the rapport

My teaching is a raft whereon men may reach the far shore. The sad fact is that so many mistake the raft for the shore.

—BUDDHA

between teacher and student. To see this kind of learning situation in your mind, forget formal classrooms and school buildings and focus on an imagined fellowship between one individual who knows and another who wishes to learn.

The time given to teaching should be released with reluctance, as time stolen from personal growth and creativity.

For the most part what a teacher receives in return is intangible. And the student shares a responsibility to make the teacher's efforts worthwhile—by attitude, by willingness to be helpful or useful. For optimal learning to occur, each partner supplies something to the other. Have you noticed how much more willing you are to help others build a wheelbarrow if they are willing to help you spade the garden? Or how much more fun it is to explore the world of geometry if the student is eager to understand?

For education to blossom, we need an atmosphere of mutual consent, without which either the student or the teacher is exploited. Why is it that we insist upon our present system of torture in school, with both the guards and the prisoners unfulfilled for an enormous segment of their lives?

Not all kids play football—why should all kids play math? The education that takes place on a ball field is voluntary. Kids can quit when they like, and coaches can refuse to work with those who don't want to be there. Those who are there, both coach and players, are there because they want to work together. Great! Let's take a lesson from the ball field and use the same approach with French, physics, music, and math. If we could be sure that all who attend classes would be as willing to play as those who play sports, what a school we would have.

VOLUNTARY LEARNING

Participation in a learning center should be voluntary, both for those who are (for this particular moment) instructors and for others who are students. If learning is to be a delight—as joyful and exciting as possible—it must occur in an atmosphere of mutual consent. Education by invitation should be the rule: no demands, no threats, no bribes.

Forced learning is violence. We may, with great difficulty, get some factual knowledge learned through authoritarian methods, but at what cost? And how terribly wasteful is coerced learning, an inefficient use of students' and instructors' time and minds. The basic learning that takes place in this situation tends to deceive both teacher and student into thinking that force is an acceptable form of communication.

Some of my own most meaningful learning sessions as a student have come about in situations where, by being helpful, I was permitted to watch, question, take part, and learn. There was the old Eskimo who let me watch him lash his sled together. Because I helped hold the thongs tight for him, he was willing to help me learn. There was a Norwegian boat builder with whom I traded labor with his cows for the opportunity to learn boat-building skills. Another time I remember plying a Japanese cooper with oranges for the pleasure and privilege of watching him work (he plied me with tea). And then there was the old, white-haired philosopher whose only "pay" came in seeing a young person as excited about his work as he was.

Sometimes it happens this way in a formal classroom, also. I liked my college German professor's classes, although working the night shift in a shipyard left me no time for study, and I did not sign up for the following term. Upon discovering my reasons for dropping the course his response was, "But you like the course, don't you? Then why don't you come anyway, even if you haven't time to do the homework?" I hope that my joy in learning was in some measure a fair return for his work as a teacher.

If learning and teaching were entirely voluntary, and if all people were considered to be potential teachers, the ridiculous current student-to-teacher ratio would settle in a much more workable equilibrium.

Learning does not need a captive audience but a captivated one. Education should be exciting enough to stand on its own merits, not needing the protection of a truant officer.

Learning is mental nourishment, and just as good food is not painful to the body, neither should learning be painful to the intellect.

When we make learning drudgery, we take away the

joy, the wonder, and the mystery. When joy vanishes, learning goes into hiding.

We learn little that is positive by being forced,
or argued at. It does little good to tell people
about the beauty in all things and the joy of feeling
sensitivity unfold. I'm convinced that we learn best from
an atmosphere or attitude that opens us
to learning. If you provide this atmosphere and embody
this attitude in your daily life, others will feel it and see
it. When the time is ripe, someone will request you to
verbalize what you've learned.

VICARIOUS LEARNING

Over the years we've taught many untruths: healing equated with bleeding; physics presuming earth to be the center of the universe; history viewed from a narrow, one-sided vantage. The algebra we learned is used by few; the poetry we learned was rarely loved and far more often hated.

We would not think of using a fifty-year-old chemistry text in a classroom. The same is true of old lessons in psychology and medicine. And think of the "truths" contained in today's textbooks, viewed fifty years hence. Isn't it ridiculous to *insist* that people study ideas and approaches that we know will soon be obsolete, especially when the chief lasting effect will be to teach people to hate learning and to feel shame and inadequacy?

Learning vicariously is an important element in our growth. We learn from others and from books in ways that speed up or shortcut the learning process; seeing examples, we learn more quickly, *but only up to a point*. Past that point we develop less and less rapidly. Each person must make a decision as to where the optimal balance between real experience and secondhand experience lies.

The Bible is an antique Volume—
Written by faded Men
At the suggestion of Holy Spectres—
Subject—Bethlehem—
Eden—the ancient Homestead—
Satan—the Brigadier—
Judas—the Great Defaulter—
David—the Troubadour—
Sin—a distinguished Precipice
Others may resist—
Boys that "believe" are very lonesome—
Other Boys are "lost"—
Had but the Tale a warbling Teller—
All the Boys would come—
Orpheus' Sermon captivated—
It did not condemn—

—EMILY DICKINSON

But choose we must or be doomed to never realize our full potential.

I'm also troubled that so much of the vicarious world of the media is sheer fabrication. Vicarious learning based upon another's true experience and honest judgment is one thing, but experience based on a commercial interest in making money through exciting our senses is another.

In most movies, TV programs, novels, and songs, we have a fake world presented—fake reality, fake love, fake anger. So much that is pouring into our lives from the media is false. Some say that we must be selective in the use of TV—I suspect this is a trap. To select wisely one has to know the choices. I choose not to use TV or newspapers, relying on books, magazines, and the shared experience of others blended with my own for mental food.

Actually, reading is both a blessing and a curse. It is one of the finest and most ingenious inventions of the human mind. Used selectively it is a marvelous aid to growth. But it can be overused until it dominates our lives, acting as a consumer of time that should be used for direct, firsthand experience. With many of us, reading is an addiction. We get the reading habit and it stifles our real lives. Aldous Huxley, a reading addict of many years' experience, called it a disease.

Freedom

An education system that tries to regiment people's minds may not do harm in every case. Some great minds have flowered in spite of despotic systems, including Victor Hugo in France, Eric Fromm in Germany, and Leo Tolstoy in Russia. But if we consider *each* mind to be a precious treasure, a unique inheritance with which we are entrusted—the greatest wealth of a culture—then the regimentation and dulling of minds must be called a crime of the first order.

Education cannot be forced or demanded. Where is a society's freedom if schooling is compulsory? Freedom is not merely a subject taught in a social studies or philosophy class. Freedom is a will-o'-the-wisp. When you seek to corner it, it flees. It is one of those subtle concepts that can be learned but cannot be taught. Freedom and tyranny are learned by the way we are treated in everyday life at home, on the street, and in the classroom. Those who make schooling compulsory are encouraging tyranny as a way of life. We cannot have it both ways. Either we approach education as a special joy, to be undertaken with care and affection, with freedom as a byproduct, or freedom will elude us and mock us.

Regimentation and forced discipline in a school undermine the basic desire to learn. The audacity and sheer stupidity of it—a democracy believing it can teach its principles and protect its interests by coercion! Creativity and conformity are opposites. Democracy thrives on creativity, while armies, prisons, and schools thrive on conformity.

You can have compulsory schooling but you cannot have compulsory education, which is an oxymoron. Trying to force people to learn is not working. Let's take a chance and instead *invite* people to learn.

Expertise?

I've been troubled by the common practice of selecting teachers for our children by what they know or appear to have studied rather than by the quality of person they are. The character, attitudes, and feelings of the guides we provide for the young are much more important than factual knowledge.

And creating an atmosphere that encourages a child to unfold and blossom is immensely more important and more difficult than presenting facts.

When students in their teens come and ask me what college they should select or what courses they should take, my response is that which school and which courses they choose matters relatively little. What matters immensely is finding the person or persons under whose guidance you enjoy learning. Most any subject can be the vehicle for expanding your knowledge of yourself and the world. How the material is presented and how you are guided, what kind of persons are your guides and how well you relate to them, these are the crucial elements.

We can learn history through art and art through history. Which we study is relatively unimportant compared with how we study and in what atmosphere.

We need to provide a rich atmosphere for children, not only rich in words and things, important as these are, but rich in experience and emotion, in unquestioning acceptance and love. I'm thinking here of a richness in *caring*.

What if teachers were simply human beings who are doing stimulating work that they enjoy and believe in, and doing this work within reach of a child's sight and hearing. Every child should have the opportunity to grow up surrounded with people who have a feeling of purpose, people who get their high out of living, who are active mentally and physically, and who demonstrate that creativity is a natural part of life.

A rich natural world is also essential. Whenever possible, children should have easy access to water—flowing water, still water, streams, surf, and storms. To hold a young child close and walk by the sea, in the forest, or in the mountains is a wonderful beginning. Dawn and dew are so often excluded from our daily lives as well as starlight and the scent of meadows.

> Many of the most important lessons in life
> can be learned but not taught.
> So, even though we cannot teach
> these experiences, we can work to create
> an atmosphere to encourage learning.

FAMILY LIFE

We need a life-centered world where the topics of conversation are real and full of meaning. Where in our present patterns of living are the opportunities for children to hear serious adult conversation, between parents or between parents and friends? This window to the adult world can be crucial in gaining perspective on life.

For children, sometimes it *is* better to be seen and not heard, to be allowed to sit and listen if they don't interrupt. This may sound anathema in our supposedly child-friendly society, but we do children a disservice by depriving them of a balanced, democratic society in which no age group is the center and where the needs of all are respected. Today a child's world is dominated by hours spent with large numbers of the same age—and the TV set.

Many families are now working so hard to give their youngsters a good "education" that they deprive them of a

---

"Believe me my young friend," said the Water Rat solemnly, *"there is nothing, absolutely nothing, half so much worth doing as simply messing about in boats—simply messing. Nothing seems really to matter—that's the charm of it. Whether you get away or whether you don't, whether you arrive at your destination or whether you reach somewhere else or whether you never get anywhere at all, you're always busy and you never do anything in particular."*

—KENNETH GRAHAME

family life. There is no replacing with money or schooling the growth that takes place in congenial and purposeful family fellowship. We rob a child doubly when we take away parental companionship and the example of seeing productive work done at home.

Give your child a parent now rather than a college education later. Spend time together—cutting the hay, planting the garden, or planning a canoe trip.

And spend more time yourself with people you respect, develop your interests, sell yourself less—all this is worth more to your child's present (and future) happiness than a college degree.

Learn to live more simply. Retire on less. Eat and drink less potato chips and beer; your paunch as well as your pocketbook will improve. Instead, make popcorn in the evening with the kids, or build a boat instead of watching the tube. As a family, do the math and see how far the money usually spent on a year's worth of cola, candy, and coffee would go toward a family trip to Canada, Canyonlands, or Chincoteague. Even suffer a little, and throw in the tea, cocktail, and tobacco money—that should make possible London, Laos, or Lambaréné.

For those who can find a way to live as a family close to nature, for even a part of the year, there are wonderful rewards for all. The opportunity for growth in facing wind and weather is tremendous. We grow in health, understanding, and security as we face the daily needs of getting food, building fires, in getting warm and dry. Short field trips are helpful; longer expeditions are marvelous.

LEARNING WITH TEENAGERS

For many adolescents in our society, life is boring and unfulfilling. School is mostly focused on intellectual achievement with little concern for feelings, the development of the heart and hands and body as well as the head.

Teenagers need to feel that they belong to something larger than themselves, a grander purpose in life beyond just making a living. The energy that goes into cliques and gangs could be refocused on building a better world—a goal that could serve as a unifying element for education in general.

What follows are some observations about elements that I have found helpful to development when built into the lives of adolescents. These also make life more pleasant for families and communities where teenagers live, serving to make a contribution to the positive growth of society.

Holistic education

We need a program that is concerned with the development of the whole person: body and mind, hands and emotions. Any educational program that does not find positive ways for the young to grow holistically is not adequate.

Adventure

The young have a tremendous thirst for the new and different, the exciting and challenging. Unless we take steps to actively build adventure and excitement into their adolescent years, the vacuum will be filled by drugs, crime, vicarious adventure through TV, and by sexual exploration in physically and mentally dangerous circumstances. Yet we can offer adventure to the young in daily life, if we choose to do so. These can be intellectual adventures, guiding them to subjects they wish to explore and learn about. Or they can be adventures in creativity, learning new skills with new materials. They can also be physical adventures, exploring mountains, caves, or the bottoms of lakes and rivers along old trade routes where lost treasures remain to be found.

Child Labor

Fire ...
Kindling
Birch bark
Flame
Wood smoke
Firelight
Embers
Hearth
Glow
Gleaming
Magic

Firemagic—
The beauty of it—
Splitting kindling was my job.
Dad came home tired—
After dark—winter—
If I forgot, he had to work longer.
I was needed.

Hold the stick with thumb tucked back.
Thunk—the hatchet falls.
Then—tump, tump, tump—
Bright cedar cleaving cleanly,
Smaller and smaller and smaller—
Halves of halves of halves.
At last—tink, tink, tink, as
Pencil-thin pieces split.

First, birch bark shreds.
Second, shavings from the shop.
Third, the lovely kindling.
Next alder sticks
And maple on top
Then with "the quick sharp scratch and blue spurt
of a lighted match"
We kindle the fire—
With gorgeous, magic, crackling flame.
"One can do worse than be" ... a splitter of kindling.

I was six. He called me "Buckshot" (moves fast and everywhere at once). Of course he saved the knotless pieces for me.

Luke

Luke—a big, tough, seventeen-year-old, with charisma—was on probation. Our school accepted him, even with his strong antipathy to teachers.

One day we played keep-away, no holds barred—little kids, teachers, boys, girls, old folks. No whistle! Play till you drop! Only one rule: if you don't have the ball they can't touch you. *No one* touched Luke, even when he had the ball. He wore *army boots*. Well, I tackled him, and was he ever surprised. Later, when I had the ball, he came on with fire in his eyes. Of course I passed the ball at the last moment, but forgot to duck. It felt like being hit by a truck. But, my body "reflexed" and as I landed on my back, my knees came up and flipped Luke about ten feet away. He admired that. He thought I'd planned it.

We were a small (actually tiny) alternative school. Just two showers. As I surreptitiously moved out ahead of the crowd, I found another pair of feet accompanying mine—in army boots. When we got to the front we raced to the showers. We hollered back and forth as we showered.

I had no towel. Luke kindly offered his. That was the beginning of a year's friendship and teamwork with Luke.

He did most everything at school (except attend classes). He fixed lights, made good bread, cut wood, cooked, and (of course) played guitar.

I was teaching an unorthodox Spanish class in preparation for study trips south, the Spanish as unorthodox as the teaching. We used songs to catch the cadence of the language, and as an anchor for vocabulary. Luke agreed to be my assistant and play while we sang. This worked well. Luke was in class, and the other kids loved it.

Luke asked to go with us to Mexico. But he had done some smuggling, knew some of the border towns, and had a strong prejudice against Mexico and things Mexican. I explained to him that border areas in many countries are poor vantage points for gaining insight into cultures.

No, I wouldn't take him with us. I had too much respect for my Mexican friends to impose him upon them. He took this well. While I was in Mexico he took over my bread baking and kept the workshop open.

After a few trips, again Luke asked to go. He said he'd never heard anyone talk about the Mexico I knew, and he wanted to get a chance to see those aspects of the country. I agreed to take him. He turned out to be one of the best and most dependable assistants I ever had. If he belayed you on a cliff in a cave you felt secure. We crawled, spelunked, and climbed across Mexico, went skin diving, explored markets, and visited crafters and ranchers. We lived with Mexican friends for a couple of weeks, each day going to work with someone in the village.

Luke got paired with Don Pablo, a mason. Small, delicately framed Don Pablo was one of my best friends, a gentle, kindly, quiet person who weighed in at about 120 pounds. What a foil for that husky, boisterous gringo kid who weighed 180. Yet Don Pablo took Luke under his wing and together they tackled the demolishing of an old adobe wall. That evening I found a very tired and cha-grined youngster. Luke had tried all day to keep up with Don Pablo while swinging a 12-pound sledge. Finally he just had to take a break and sit down, though Don Pablo just kept swinging. Then this smiling, lightweight, forty-year-old Mexican took the now humbled Luke home and treated him to the feast of his life.

I was happy. We had a new Luke with a new appreciation of Mexico.

Travel

Travel has almost universal appeal. Geographical exploration with young people is one of the most exciting keys to their growth. They will work hard to learn the material needed for a trip, whether this involves writing letters, making equipment, or learning a language. The "rolling" or expeditionary learning center is a little used tool that has returns in education which far outweigh the effort expended. Expensive? No! Costs can be lower than staying at home. Discipline? That depends on the attitude of the leader and the size of the group. If you want to be with the students and they want to be with you—again, schooling through freely chosen associations—discipline is not a big problem. Groups of five or six kids with one or two adults is about ideal. The dynamics of larger groups making minute-by-minute and day-to-day decisions is more cumbersome and less productive.

Beauty

We need to examine the visual surroundings of the young. Our present school buildings are, by and large, institutional architecture designed for ease of maintenance and as impressive public buildings rather than to aid the growth of the inmates. Dominated by corridors, and lockers, they have high ceilings and fluorescent lighting, with hard, cold, easily cleaned surfaces, which also make them acoustically harsh. Rooms are commonly giant-sized cubes. Such impersonal architecture is not conducive to optimal student growth.

Imagine schools so cozy, so personal and varied, that we would have difficulty distinguishing them from homes; smaller spaces, elimination of corridors, students in much smaller groups, lots of nooks and crannies and private spaces, soft quiet floor coverings and shoeless occupants.

(The complaints of the janitor about dirt on the carpet can be eliminated by students and teachers leaving their spaces neat and clean as part of the learning program, as their contribution to bread labor.) The learning center will ideally be built by the students and the community in general, ensuring a gaining of building skills, a closer relationship among those who will use the center, and a greater feeling of care and responsibility for the building.

It would be lovely to see a learning center where affection and beauty were everywhere—in the objects within the space—in the space itself—in the people invited to take part—with the beauty of discovery pervading the whole.

When Emily Dickinson was a little girl, she was told that in the woods she might be kidnapped by goblins, bitten by a snake or poisoned by a flower. Instead, she says she met only angels, who were far shyer of her than she was of them.

—GENEVIEVE TAGGARD

Yurts: Learning by Doing

The full magic of yurt design first struck me in 1962 when *National Geographic* (in the March issue) published a William O. Douglass article on Mongolia. This piece included a series of photos showing the erection and covering of a yurt. I was impressed by the native genius of the nomads of central Asia, who had discovered that by the use of a tension band to take the outward thrust of the roof, a conical tent could be raised onto a circular wall and achieve a spacious, economical structure—one of the most efficient surface-to-volume structures ever devised. The beauty of the engineering was instantly apparent: the lack of tie beams, lintels, headers, and joists; the hyperbolic paraboloid walls and conical roof all held in dynamic tension by that woven band at the eaves; the central skylight for light and ventilation.

My initial response to the problem of adapting yurt design to our climate was to cross the roof poles in a strengthening lattice while eliminating the complex central roof ring of the native yurt. Steel cable is a modern material with very appealing strength-to-cost ratio, and so began forty years of experiments blending steel tension bands with lumber and glass in circular dwellings. During this time we have built some three hundred modern yurts, varying in size from small playhouses to structures of sixty feet in diameter with three and four floors. They range in setting and climate from Florida to Alaska and as far afield as Turkey, New Zealand, and Japan. They are in use as homes, as school buildings, and as workshops. Modern yurts have also been used as mountain shelters, guest cabins at resorts, greenhouses, libraries, saunas, and teen retreats. Sometimes a central yurt is surrounded by a group of satellite yurts for a diversity of uses; these may be independent structures or joined to the main yurt by hallways or breezeways.

Just as important as the fun and excitement of designing new forms from ancient principles has been the pleasure of using the construction of these designs as a vehicle for communicating with people about Social Design. My chief concern since the mid-1950s has been seeking ways to get more people involved in building a better society, one that works for all people everywhere and that respects the planet. Lecturing and writing are fine in their way, but I feel that the crisis we are in requires more effectual means to help people see how crucial it is to be personally involved in designing better ways of living. Building our own homes can be an important factor in developing a greater intimacy with that piece of the world that plays such a dominant role in our lives.

R. Ellis

Nature

As much as possible, closeness to nature should be incorporated into the life of the young through the learning center. There should be orchards and gardens and wild lands available.

Groups can go out and explore the natural world and learn how to be safe and happy in all weather and seasons. Students must be given an opportunity to learn that nature is not an enemy but a potential friend that needs only to be understood to be helpful. Admittedly, it may not be wise to attempt too close a relationship with a tornado or an avalanche, yet with proper guidance and gear, people of all ages can learn to cope with storms, with extremes of heat and cold, and to enjoy these challenges.

Moonlight can also be as conducive to learning as sunlight. To study trees by moonlight leads to an awareness of shape, design, and detail usually ignored in full daylight.

In a society with a such widespread emotional insecurity, an intimate and personal contact with nature can serve as a sea anchor in times of emotional storm.

Community

In most schools, the surrounding community is too infrequently used as a resource for learning. Local people can greatly enrich the educational program by teaching, demonstrating skills, or talking with groups. Everyone is a potential resource person—those who have traveled, craftspeople, homemakers, engineers, boat builders, gardeners, nurses. Not only does any community have an abundance of expertise just waiting to be tapped, but in a true community-based learning center, all kinds of talent would grow, through the activities of the program, into new possibilities of resource people.

WHAT IS HE?

— A man of course.
Yes, but what does he do?
— He lives and is a man.
Oh quite, but he must work?
He must have a job of some sort.
— Why?
Because obviously he is not
  one of the leisured classes.
— I don't know. He has lots of leisure
  and he makes quite beautiful chairs.
There you are then. He's a chair maker.
—Oh no!
Anyhow a carpenter and a joiner.
— Not at all.
But you said so.
— What did I say?
That he made chairs and
  was a joiner and a carpenter.
— I said he made chairs, but I
  did not say he was a carpenter.
All right then. He's just an amateur.
— Perhaps. Would you say a thrush was a
  professional flutist or just an amateur?
I'd say it was just a bird.
— And I say he is just a man.
All right! You always did quibble.

—D.H. Lawrence

63

This is likely an idiosyncrasy of mine,
but one that keeps nudging to be let out:
The criteria for concentrating on certain areas for
educational exploration should be based upon how
this activity is related to the building of a better world.
In these critical times, we cannot afford the luxury
of any other focus. We so badly need a focal point
for our energies, and this is one that can make all
people know that they are needed.
We will have a better world only when we
as individuals start choosing to spend our time
on those pursuits that we believe will help
move us toward that goal.

Civilization Needs Redefinition

At this time little encouragement seems to be given to doing original work—doing work that has not been done before. An original project may be as simple as trying a new variety of seed that has never been tried in the school's climate before or as complicated as building a school of yurts (as was done in New Hampshire). With truly original endeavors, there is no guarantee that the experiment will work. No matter. What is important is the spirit of the enterprise and the possibility that the students may turn up some useful knowledge.

Projects in which students do original work can be wonderful learning aids, fostering feelings of usefulness and self-confidence. Originality can add flavor, excitement—leaven to the loaf. Even if originality is not the daily fare in schools, it is important nonetheless to build room for original work into our educational programs, to encourage and honor creative thinking so this ability can flower and never be lost.

Original work is not hard to build into programs, yet the difficulty lies in overcoming the inertia that exists in regard to the new and unfamiliar, as well as uncertainty due to lack of experience on the instructors' parts.

Building original work into a program can be done with positive results from kindergarten through graduate school. (Sadly, many doctoral students are still jumping through academic hoops. What a loss to them personally and to society as a whole that they were never guided during their student years into work that is exciting, creative, and a benefit to humanity.)

All too often the emphasis in school is on the *what* of learning, while neglecting the *how*—the manner in which we learn, the intellectual climate, the atmosphere, the actual learning space, and the quality of people who are our guides.

This *how* may turn out to be the most crucial factor in the learning equation. If we can create an atmosphere conducive to learning, we set the stage for the enjoyment of learning. The person who has discovered this joy then has the opportunity to absorb knowledge in any one of myriad directions.

This is such a contrast to our normal method of stuffing the student with unappreciated knowledge, with a resultant allergic reaction to learning in general. And that is a very persistent allergy once acquired. What a waste.

The human mind is our greatest treasure, our finest possession. Accordingly, the growth and development of the mind deserves to be sought with all of the fervor, diligence, and dedication with which we sought the poles and the moon. Recognition of this is our most urgent problem. We need the fullest functioning of as many minds as we can muster if we are to avoid the impending social and ecological crisis.

That which is harmful to you,
do not do to another.
That is the whole law.
The rest is mere commentary.

—HILLEL, 100 B.C.

NONVIOLENCE: A GENTLE REVOLUTION

Nonviolence has come to be known chiefly through the writings and actions of Mahatma Gandhi in the struggle to free India from foreign rule. For Gandhi, the term "nonviolence" had a much broader meaning than contained in its use in politics. He saw nonviolence as a primary element in human relationships.

Inherent in the word "violence" is *violation*, the invasion of someone's (or something's) aura, space, territory. We tend to think of violence as a physical attack, but this is only part of the meaning of violence. At the root of all violation there is the crime of disrespect. All wrong stems from this. When we act without regard for the spirit or nature of a thing, we violate it. To the extent that we become sensitive to that nature or spirit, violence will tend to disappear.

I would like to become kinder and gentler to the spirit of all things.

Our most important duty is to seek to know—to understand. Only with knowledge can we do right. Good intentions are necessary, but without knowledge they founder on ignorance.

Prejudice, one of the ugliest, most hateful, and most violent of conditions, causes much of the misery in the world. Prejudice is a poison that injures both the giver and the receiver. It is urgent that we discover ways of life that are not bought at the expense of another—ways that do not exploit, do not diminish other people. We need to find a positive way out of the insecurity that makes us feel so small and afraid that we have to degrade others to raise our self-esteem.

When happy and emotionally secure, we have no need to put others down. Knowledge, combined with emotional security, helps to destroy prejudice, which cannot withstand the combined onslaught of light and health.

If we will listen carefully and with care to our opponents, trying to understand from where they speak, learning and movement become more possible—for both of us. If my adversaries know that I care, that I believe their troubles are my troubles, that we are one and not separate, and that I too am searching and need their perspectives, a more fertile soil for communication is produced.

FREEDOM

Freedom and knowledge are inextricably woven together. Freedom has been described as ending where a neighbor's nose begins. Unlimited freedom does not exist outside of the imagination, and we need knowledge to know the boundaries—that is, where my neighbor's nose does in fact begin—the distance being much longer if I am running a paper mill than if I am planting a garden.

Through relations with our fellows, we find freedom limited in certain directions (bells cannot be rung at midnight with impunity), yet greatly expanded in others (freedom to read is enhanced by someone having written a book).

The fear of ridicule drives us to the worst kinds of cowardice. How many of the young, greatly aspiring, have had their aspirations pricked like bubbles by the single word "Utopia," and by the fear of passing for visionaries in the eyes of sensible people?

—ANDRÉ GIDE

To know and not to do is not to know.

—Wang Yang Ming

Freedom without responsibility is license. In our society, there is great confusion about the concept of freedom, and it is of utmost importance that the difference be clearly seen. We have people feeling they can do what they like with their "own" land, not realizing that their actions may injure someone else in another place and time. Cutting trees to clear mountain land may cause flooding for a neighbor downstream and cause "my" soil to be washed away, destroying the birthright of another generation. We should be free to nurture and to care for but not to destroy. True freedom does not harm others.

Gandhi said, "If we are to be non-violent, we must not wish for anything on this earth which the meanest and lowest of human beings cannot have." He believed that if those of us who are wealthy with possessions and knowledge and freedom would choose to live as simply as the poorest, there would be no despised lower class, and the whole society would improve. Gandhi had a genius for seeing clearly through a jumble of social conditions to the central issue.

We need a movement that will do for nurture and
nonviolence what in the past has been done for
prejudice, hatred, nationalism, and war.

Ideals are the Faery Oil
With which we help the wheel.

—Emily Dickinson

Ideals

Down through the years there has been much resentment and ridicule of those who have sought to live a nonviolent life. Many people have been deterred from aiming as high as they might have aimed out of fear of jeering, with accusations of "Utopian," "Purist," "Perfectionist," "Idealist."

But often all that is needed is a kind word or a friendly hand on the shoulder to keep the seeker on the quest. And though the good life is forever out of reach, the attempt to reach it is important.

What if our only goal could be perfection? We should seek nothing less. For me, perfection is achieved through developing a nurturing attitude: in being to others as is soil, water, and sunlight to a flower—making no demands, seeking no return, asking only to be of service to help loveliness to flourish, with confidence in the developing beauty that is the basic nature of the organism.

67

We need to face the prejudice against utopian thinking and seek to live honestly—nonviolently—without harming others, if the society we seek is ever to be more than a dream. Transformation of the whole society begins within each of us. The Buddha said that the road from darkness into light is long, and those first, small steps along the path of utmost importance. Each of us must take those first, small steps if we are to do our best to create a happy society.

HIDDEN VIOLENCE

If we are to root out violence and exploitation in the world around us, we must seek out those symbols in language and daily life that reinforce violence and create alternatives for these.

For example, if we believe that the arts of a culture reflect the essential nature of that culture, then it behooves us to examine the art, music, and architecture produced by totalitarian, paternalistic, tyrannical, and democratic societies and compare them.

Luxuries are especially seductive. Like drugs they are habit-forming and socially dangerous, their full effects often unrecognized and unsuspected. Karl Marx called religion the opiate of the masses. We are now living in an era when opiates have become the religion of the masses: the opiates of television, nationalism, technology, and consumption.

When we admire a full-rigged ship, are we aware of the tyrannical society that existed aboard? Could a Gothic cathedral have been produced by an emotionally secure, democratic society? Or is the fear of hell necessary to make such an edifice possible? Knowing that "civilization" with all its violence caused this or that manifestation of art to be produced, we must examine our civilization to see if its cultural achievements also have the disease of violence and need healing.

As there are both violent and peaceful forms of art, music, government, work, architecture, design, child

J. Allen

Perfection
To seek to be to another
As sunlight and water
To a flower
As humus and air
Asking no returns
Making no demands
Encouraging no direction
Asking only the privilege
Of helping it to blossom

care—in fact, of all forms of culture—should we not measure the success of a civilization by the ascent of peaceful forms over violent ones? What would the architecture of a truly democratic society look like? Or the music? Or the painting?

WE TEACH WHAT WE ARE

In the time of George Fox, people commonly relied on the priesthood's interpretation of the Bible. Fox made a revolutionary challenge to his neighbors and parishioners: "What dost *thou* think?"

Here was a startling, unsettling suggestion that one's own thoughts might be valid and bear consideration. Because what we think greatly affects what we do, and what we do affects what we think, of equal importance is, "What dost thou *do*?" Can our deeds be beautiful? The Shaker Margaret Melcher wrote of "the beauty that comes unsought when lives are right."

In modern parlance, "We teach what we are." The art of living is the most important of the arts. All others derive from this. Without a vision of a beautiful life, the other arts are incomplete.

Which is more important, beautiful things or a beautiful life? We need vigilance if these two outlooks are not to compromise one another, for instance, wanting to live a nonviolent life while holding a violent concept of beauty.

I remember a lovely formal garden at a famed university, with sheltering walls, a sunken courtyard with a fountain, flowers in bloom from early spring to late fall, very secluded, with ancient yews. I was given the opportunity to build a small, round study for myself in that garden. As time passed I realized that the garden was kept in order by a small army of gardeners, people who were not accepted as users but only as workers. The garden

My Soul—accused me—And I quailed—
As Tongues of Diamond had reviled
All else accused me—and I smiled—
My Soul—that Morning—was My Friend—

Her favor—is the best Disdain
Toward Artifice of Time—or Men—
But her Disdain—'twere lighter bear
A finger of Enamelled Fire.

—EMILY DICKINSON

lost much of its appeal for me, whereas such a garden, if cooperatively built and cared for by those who use it, would be a delight.

In seeking to build a better world, we need to be alert that our energies may be drained into side issues that miss the main problems facing society. It is so seductive—so much easier—to have an antagonist. We need to find ways to fight the problems themselves and not other people. By fighting someone, we create other problems,

Democratic Architecture

It may sound strange to talk of honest and dishonest houses. After all, aren't houses neutral, material objects? Yet if a house is larger than we can build and care for on our own, it could be regarded as violent, exploitative architecture.

The larger and more complicated the house we build, the more that house becomes a time-consuming luxury, requiring effort that could be focused on areas of greater need and worth.

Balance in this, as in all matters, takes judgment. Some people put in a disproportionate amount of time styling their hair, some spend hours on their car, some are obsessed with their tennis stroke, and some of us are inclined to spend too much time on our houses.

Until there is a decent balance of basic necessities for all people, we are duty-bound not to waste time and energy on peripheral things. The modern yurt has been designed as part of the quest for a democratic architecture—a shelter that people can take part in building for themselves. For this to be possible, it must be simple, take relatively little time to build, be aesthetically pleasing, low in cost, and easily cleaned and maintained.

There will not be one form of structure that answers the needs of all people. Climate, occupation, and taste vary too greatly for universal rules. We need to experiment with many designs using many different materials. And we need to design not for material gain but to create the best, most genuinely nonviolent architecture possible.

What are your requirements for a democratic house?

generating hatred and anger—exchanging one prejudice for another. These are poisons that maim and kill, just as guns and clubs do, and often create problems deeper and harder to solve.

The individualized or separate equal rights that some groups are seeking may not be worth much when attained. What is the value of having equal rights to mediocrity? We need a uniting of forces. To create a nonviolent society will require the energy of conscientious people everywhere. Without this pulling together we may end up with no society at all. The forces of money and power, of prejudice and violence, are happy to see our energies fragmented. We need a superior world concept to be equal in. Let us seek to grow beyond provincialism and partisanship and work together, joining with people of like mind and ideals—rather than like sex, age, religion, color, or nationality—to design a new society in its entirety.

PREJUDICE: A POISON

Prejudice is often deeply seated and exceedingly resistant to change. A possible cure lies in recognizing the nature of prejudice, in summoning a desire to change, and increasing our knowledge and our physical and emotional security so that we are able to view the world with a clearer eye. Prejudice toward other peoples, cultures, or religions may be expressed in actions that seem small when viewed as individual acts, but collectively these constitute an evil tide that engulfs us and makes it possible to go to war with one another, reinforcing an ever more vicious circle.

The essence of nonviolence is in attitude. An understanding of this importance of attitude has great ramifications for the shaping of a better world. We are in great need of people who are sensitive to needs, to issues, to problems, with the ability to analyze intelligently and to arrive at workable solutions. What could be better training than becoming aware of the basic design—the true nature—of the world around us?

Each time we find a way to live more simply, we aid others in two ways: we use less of the world's resources for our own lives; and we help set an example for those who are now striving to copy the affluent life of their neighbors. The greater the striving for affluence, the more wretched will be the poor and the greater will be the chasm between the haves and the have-nots. Violence will be inevitable.

Teaching Children Violence

We teach children brutality with the media, with "histories," with toys, and with military training. We feed them a steady (heady) diet of violence in their most formative years and expect them to grow into gentle, sensitive, loving adults. It simply cannot be done.

The violence of wars and urban rioting is minor compared to the scale of the violence that goes on every day in the lives of small children. We destroy creativity, spontaneity, and confidence; we stifle curiosity, sensitivity, and a sense of wonder; we kill love.

Out of this daily stifling, warping, and crippling of a child's potential grows an insecure, fearful, unhappy, and hate-ridden society in which prejudice, crime, and war are not only possible but the norm.

Consciously working to design a better society and encouraging creativity to flower has a multiplying effect, for if it's true (as asserted in the standard formulation of psychology) that "increase in creativity is sublimation of aggression," then helping people to express their creativity reduces their need for aggression.

More ways are needed for larger numbers of people to have their concerns heard. Smaller social and political groupings help to make this possible as do smaller classes in our schools.

Vigilance

When Wendell Phillips said, "Eternal vigilance is the price of liberty," he might well have been contemplating language instead of politics. We must be vigilant with our language if we are not to be heedless bystanders as the manipulators work their will.

Being sensitive to the positive and negative aspects of authority is extremely important at this time as we search for clues for creating a better social design. Many of our words are in constant transition, sometimes by unconscious cultural change and sometimes by conscious manipulation. We need to be on the alert for this and reexamine crucial words.

"Civilization" and "primitive" are two words that require reevaluation. With respect to culture, "primitive" is often used to mean backward, inferior, undeveloped, or uncivilized, whereas "civilized" is used to mean the opposite: a higher, better way of life and one that is more advanced.

We use "primitive" to refer to a culture that we consider to be uncivilized and also use the term for someone who is violent or brutal. Yet some allegedly primitive cultures have very little violence—for example, the Lapps, Eskimos, or Tarahumara Indians—while many civilized cultures are often engaged in wars of annihilation—consider Rome, Germany, the United States.

We call ourselves civilized though we spend more on weaponry than any society has ever done. This hypocrisy, a form of self-deception, is dangerous. Hypocrisy keeps us from truly knowing ourselves, the first stage in

The rule of no realm is mine, but all worthy things that are in peril as the world now stands, those are in my care. And for my part I shall not wholly fail in my task if anything passes through the night that can still grow fair or bear fruit and flower again in the days to come. For I, too, am a steward. Did you not know?

—J. R. R. Tolkien

growing to individual and cultural maturity. So, eternal vigilance is also the price of our continual growth and maturing.

> To "kill time" is to kill part of our potential.
> The amount of wisdom that we are able to accumulate
> and to generate—to glean, garner, or scratch
> together—by the time we are, say, eighty—to have
> available for sharing with the world—is directly
> reduced by the amount of time we have killed.

LANGUAGE AS ENVIRONMENT

Of all the beautiful inventions of humankind, language is perhaps foremost, a fitting symbol of the folk genius of our ancient ancestors. We should treat this inheritance gently, tenderly, with love and affection, with respect and admiration, like an elderly friend.

We live in a time when language is casually treated and greatly abused, perhaps to our peril. Language is not a plaything but a primary element in our lives, central to our being and well-being. To the extent that we use language casually, disrespectfully, and meanly, there is danger that it may backfire and do us harm.

Imagine language being to us as water is to a fish—an all-surrounding, all but invisible environment, taken for granted, mostly unnoticed but crucial, delicate, easily polluted, and damaged unless given care. Language may be as vital an element in our lives as air and water; if so, we pollute it at our peril. I am troubled, for example,

by the current use of obscenities—words that debase life—and troubled that phrases associated with sex and elimination have become expletives expressing anger and derision. To the extent that we misuse elementary life functions—in act, in word, or in attitude—we foul our own spring.

When we misuse language we violate it. When we deprecate the body or sex in our speech, we lessen the wonder and beauty they can hold for us. And even though a holder of the highest office in the land used the term "asshole" to denigrate someone, need we stoop to the level of presidents? Using a word for part of the body to degrade another is offensive, showing immaturity and lack of sensitivity to the beauty of the body. No part of the body is ugly—it is the misuse of life that is ugly.

We need a reverence for language as well as for all forms of life.

In addition to debasing human life, we frequently degrade other forms of life. We use the words "beast," "pig," "rat," "dog," or "bitch" with the intention of putting another down. But are we so unhappy, so sick, and so insecure that we need to gain a feeling of superiority by putting other creatures down? We violate the spirit of these creatures and of all life when we use them carelessly to describe qualities we dislike in each other.

I believe that each time we violate the spirit of something else, we violate our own.

Witless Knitting, or The Adventures of a Knitwit

The reindeer pulled up to the log house. We stomped off the snow and entered. My driver said a few words to the ancient woman seated by the window, then told me that the craftsman I was seeking would return soon and that I should wait. The woman stared out the window, ignoring me, obviously ill at ease with this stranger in the house. It seemed best to put her at ease by ignoring her in return.

So I sat down on a wall bench across the room and pulled out my "knitting"—I use this term for want of a better term in English—which is a type of weaving practiced in odd corners of the world and done with one needle, a sort of complex "darning" whereby the initiated can make mittens, caps, slippers, and so on. The Norwegians call it *nålbinding;* the Swedes, *soma;* and I prefer "witless knitting."

Now, if there is anything an elderly Lapp woman knows it is fiber arts. If it can be done with yarn, she knows it and knows it well. This is her turf.

The first remedy for our social impasse was to have her see a *man* using yarn. "Well, here is a curiosity," I could just about hear her thinking. Second, this was a technique new to her. She could tell instantly by my hand motions that here was a different way to use yarn. I kept my eyes down and continued to make my mitten.

I have found from long experience that when traveling to remote areas of the world there is always a need to wait for planes, trains, boats, dogsleds, or reindeer *pulkas,* and life is much more relaxed if one keeps a notebook and some hand work ready, along with a bit of food and a sleeping bag.

This was too much for the good dame's curiosity. After about twenty minutes she was looking over my shoulder. Unperturbed, I continued weaving. Then I looked up and smiled. She smiled back. I slowed down the stitching to enable her to see. Then I passed the mitten to her to try.

Back and forth it went. Her nimble fingers and mind soon had the technique. After a few hours, when her son returned, we were fast friends, and yet we had not a single word in common.

Weaving from Swedish Lappland.

73

LOVE THY NEIGHBOR

"Thou shalt love thy neighbor as thyself . . ."
As much as I love myself?
I did not understand.
Then it happened:
Could that possibly mean
Love thy neighbor as a part of thyself?
Suddenly it came alive: a rule to live by.

My neighbor and I are one—as fingers of one hand
My neighbor's welfare is my welfare—
His poverty my poverty,
His happiness my happiness.

Time passed.
The old commandment has grown to mean
Love thy planet as a part of thyself.
Treat it with love and kindness,
With care, gentleness, and thanksgiving.
Any harm done to my planet
Is harm done to me.

BELONGING-NESS

This individual self—this *me*—is made up of increments from many sources, including the support, encouragement, and thoughts that our friends contribute. These contributions are a vital part of what we are. Who of us cannot remember a time when the encouragement of a friend changed our life by giving us the courage to continue? At such a moment, this friend became part of you.

In a larger sense, look at all of the gifts that you have received through the thoughts of others—all that you've read or heard or seen expressed—the examination of which has brought new understanding. Many people are apt to take sole credit for these ideas, but are they ever wholly *ours*? Are we not the bud on the tree, the momentary blossoming of all the effort that has gone into the roots and bark, sap and leaves?

This analogy encompasses our belonging-ness to, and dependency upon, the water, air, sunlight, and nutrients we need to think, to grow, to act. In this sense there is a body beyond the social body that is also an intimate part of us—this is the world and universe around us. When someone plows a hill and lets the topsoil wash away, part of me is scarred and damaged as well.

If I feel so concerned about other forms of life, why am I not a vegetarian? Somehow I have never been able to take the anthropocentric position of putting animal life on a higher plane than plant life by eating plants and refusing to eat animals. From there it is easy to set humans up as the highest of the animals, which seems a dangerous step to take. We are different from other animals, and from plants and stones and water. We are not any better than they are, only different—wonderfully different.

It is painful to choose to destroy anything—be it plant

or animal, living or nonliving—but life demands destruction. We—plants and animals—are all interdependent; we take away and we give back. The least we can do is not to wantonly destroy, to use as little as need be, and to cultivate a reverence for all things, then to ask that our remains be gratefully returned to the cycle.

Anthropocentrism reinforces a false position. In our insecurity, elevating humanity bolsters our ego, as we try to see ourselves at the top of the evolutionary ladder. Wouldn't it be better to gain our security from a sense of partnership and belonging-ness, of kinship with the other forms around us? False feelings of superiority impede our understanding of one another, of life, and of nature.

Down through the ages has come a plea that we revere life. This greatly needed and seldom-heeded admonition was given added emphasis by the voice of Albert Schweitzer. I want us to go further along that pathway— to seek to develop a reverence for all things as well as for life in the broader sense—for the land and water and air, for tools and houses and a bowl that has been made with care, patience, and skill.

Erich Fromm spoke of the necessity of "love—care, respect, and responsibility" for our fellows. I want to learn to extend that care, respect, and responsibility to all things as well as to fellow humans, and not only to a deer and a birch tree, but also to a stone, a stream, and the sky. Not that we shouldn't use a stone, but we should use whatever we use with reverence, with concern for its nature, beauty, and spirit.

A Pair of Huaraches

One afternoon in the mid-1950s I was wandering through the market in a small town in Jalisco in search of *huaraches,* that marvelous woven Mexican footgear that is neither quite shoe nor quite sandal.

It was close to siesta time when I managed to locate some fine ones in a small booth at the back of the market.

The vendor was bright eyed, cheerful, and beguiling as only a ten-year-old Mexican girl can be. So charmed was I by this delightful entrepreneur that I would have gladly given her any price she asked. But—to play the game out, in the accepted fashion—I would bargain first.

"What are you asking for this pair of *huaraches?*"
"Twenty-five pesos."

"I'll give you twenty."
"Eighteen."
(As I began to giggle internally):"Seventeen."
"Sixteen."
"Fifteen."
"Fourteen."

At this point, I could hold it in no longer and cracked up. The little girl gasped, putting her hand over her mouth, and dashing out the back abandoned her wares. This was her first experience on the selling side.

Her mother appeared, thoroughly enjoying the humor of the situation. I paid her the asking price, happy in having received much more than a pair of *huaraches.*

I ask that we seek to develop Fromm's "personal, intimate, kinship relationship" with the world.

PEACEFUL GRAVES

We show ignorance of our kinship with nature by our burial practices. Are we so afraid of becoming one with the earth that we need to fill dead bodies with poisons and seal them away in caskets to slow their return to the soil? To deny our nature in this way demonstrates a fundamental insecurity and lack of appreciation for life and its cycles.

How much more beautiful it would be to ease the body's transition to compost, in the process helping the earth's green carpet to bloom. Let us plant trees on graves, turning our graveyards into parks and orchards and forests. If I cannot be the spirit in the tree, at least let me help the tree's spirit to flourish. Peter Freuchen tells of an Eskimo sitting on his grandmother's grave trying to absorb some of her wisdom. What a beautiful idea! What a fine setting for the absorption of the essence of Grandmother's spirit.

If dead things love, if earth and water distinguish friends from enemies, I should like to possess their love. I should like the green earth not to feel my step as a heavy burden. I should like her to forgive that she for my sake is wounded by plow and harrow, and willingly to open for my dead body. And I should like the waves, whose shining mirror is broken by my oars, to have the same patience with me as a mother has with an eager child when it climbs upon her knee, careless of the uncrumpled silk of her dress.

—SELMA LAGERLOFF

Elder Frederick thought it would be appropriate to have "a tree planted by every grave, that thus death would lose its sting, the grave its victory over the living, and the fear of death be supplanted by a spirit of rejoicing." And besides he felt that it was only right to return the favor of life to the earth: "Each human being, having been comforted and benefited by the scenery thus furnished while living, would add to the earth's fertility and beauty by the deposit of a body for which he no longer had any use."

—JUNE SPRIGG

*Call not that riches which may be lost; virtue is our true
wealth and the true reward of the possessor. It cannot
be lost, and will not abandon us unless life itself first
leaves us.*

—Leonardo da Vinci

WEALTH, RICHES, TREASURE

I remember the joy I felt as a child, finding in the toe of my Christmas stocking a wonderful orange, almost too precious to eat. Or when someone brought a new record home, everyone eagerly listened to it. Now fruit and recordings are commonplace.

I want to live in such a way that small gifts are meaningful.

In a society that has too much material wealth, it becomes increasingly difficult to find a gift to give that is both simple and needed. Here in the wilderness, where everything has to be carried in by pack or by canoe, small things take on greater significance.

It is unfortunate that the word "wealth" has been co-opted, so that in common usage wealth refers to money or to those things that money can buy—material possessions. To be successful is to be wealthy. Yet many people also feel that to be successful is to be fulfilled.

Is it possible to have too much material wealth?
And is it possible to have a life with too much leisure—
as harmful as one with too much toil?

The Example of the Rich

Imagine a society of a thousand people each having a yearly income of $1,000 and living in poverty. Then imagine that one person in that community has an income ten times the average. If this money were divided evenly, it would mean only $10 more per year for each person. This 1 percent increase would help somewhat,

---

If wealth and fame do in the mind abide,
then naught but dust is all your yellow gold.

—from a Chinese poem

---

but not a great deal. Although a fairer sharing of the world's wealth is urgently necessary, merely redistributing monetary wealth is minuscule in importance compared with the need for intelligent, cooperative action aimed at improving the quality of life.

The wealth of the rich would not mean much if it were spread out evenly, but the example *of luxurious living spread about is a time bomb.*

The great evil of the rich is the example they set. Yet the power of the rich is very fragile, for their privilege cannot withstand the gaze of an enlightened populace. What good is their accumulated "wealth" if we refused to work for them? If we refused to accept their values and their way of life?

The trap we are in is that we want to emulate the rich. Their factories produce for us, and we are their buyers, the consumers. If we refused to buy junk, they would have to produce quality. A factory is a liability if its products won't sell. They will produce whatever we demand. We have the control—though we don't know it yet—whenever we decide to take responsibility: that is, when we become mature in our economic thinking and in the use of our purchasing power. The monetary power of the wealthy is a social disease that can be cured, but the remedy needs our help.

We now have a class of people living according to a consumption pattern that exceeds that of the monarchs of previous centuries and that is rapidly devouring the world's finite resources. It might not matter, physically, if a few thousand people acted in such adolescent fashion, but when millions do, the effect will ultimately be catastrophic, with the added danger that more millions, seeing the example of the rich, will strive for this luxury as well.

That is our greatest danger now, and the crisis is ap-

It is well that thou givest bread to the hungry, but better were it that none hungered and that thou haddest none to give.

—Augustine

proaching epidemic proportions. From this vantage point, the "voluntary simplicity" of Richard Gregg becomes more important than ever before. Is it possible that we, the people of the industrial nations, the leaders in the race to destroy the earth, could set the pace for a move in a positive direction? Can we meet the challenge?

Whatever we do is watched closely by the poor of the world. Will we use our economic advantage for the good of humankind or will we continue to rob and to exploit?

We must search for ways to live that are within the grasp of all people. In this light, redefining wealth and riches becomes a primary challenge.

Success

If I stock up possessions at the expense of my neighbors, I commit robbery, for until there is enough for all, surplus is theft from those who don't have enough. And if I say, "I am involvéd in mankinde," and I express respect and care for the social body around me, my definitions of success are in conflict, because monetary success is opposed to the well-being of my social body.

We need to make clear our definition of "wealth." The word has different meanings for different people, and we often use it to connote widely varying concepts.

It has been helpful to me to break the idea of wealth into three categories:

— Destructive, violent, or false wealth
— Neutral wealth
— Creative, productive, or nonviolent wealth

Destructive or violent wealth includes those possessions that enrich one at the expense of others. This includes monetary wealth and material possessions that are in such limited supply that by owning them we deprive others. This is exploitative wealth, usually acquired through competition, theft, warfare, or inheritance, and protected by the law with its threat of violence. Wealth of this kind is usually dependent on finite resources. Although masquerading under the title of "riches," this kind of wealth is in reality poverty, in relation to our social body. An exploitative rich person *restricts* the flow of what is valuable instead of being a creator of wealth.

Neutral wealth comprises those possessions that neither help nor hinder other people. Under this heading I would place private learning (enjoyment of study for its own sake), things made for one's own use, playing music for personal enjoyment, or collecting materials that are not in limited supply such as rocks, sea shells, or folk songs.

Creative or productive wealth includes all those possessions with which you enrich others. This includes knowledge that is shared, talents or skills that are used for the benefit of others, and those unique and wonderful realms of wealth wherein the more you give of them the larger grows your store. Chief among these are love and friendship, along with kindness and care, enthusiasm, health, and joy. Shared music is doubly enriching.

Creative wealth is nonviolent, based on sharing. To acquire this form of wealth no one need live on the back of another.

Each of us must ask, "What does the word *success* mean for me?" We will need to do this repeatedly if we are to live a life that does not exploit others. To the extent that our daily life aids society as a whole to succeed, we raise the base of our own individual success or well-being. We need to move beyond today's tawdry, shortsighted, destructive "success," which is cultural suicide.

GIVING

Perhaps it helps to approach such an emotionally loaded topic as wealth obliquely, to examine ways in which wealth affects us personally, in our daily lives.

What are *your* treasures? What are *your* jewels? What are the sources of *your* creative wealth? Contemplation of these questions is important to individuals and to society. Searching for your treasures and bringing them into the parlor of your mind can give great pleasure while helping to rid the world of a violent, destructive concept of wealth. With understanding, violent wealth can be made to disappear as a valid concept.

One facet of being rich is to be able to give gifts. No matter how much we manage to store up material possessions, if we are unable to give, we are poor.

What are the gifts that do not require a hoarding of possessions, that do not require the exploitation of others? The answer is things that cost little but are pleasing to both giver and receiver: a poem or a piece of music that we feel will bring pleasure; a shared meal, or a recipe; knowledge of a lovely spring, or a way to make shoes that are simple, beautiful, and comfortable; a gift of time, for helping plant an apple tree, dig a foundation, or care for a child.

The finest gifts depend on thoughtfulness, sensitivity, knowledge, and caring—not on the material wealth of the giver. Is there a finer gift than receiving a lovely person as a neighbor or friend?

FASHION

A more generous way of defining wealth requires rethinking many aspects of our lives: our dress, our homes, our way of living. Rather than rare paintings and china, why not fill our homes with the presence of joy, evidence of the search for wisdom, and signs of caring? Are not

It is the ancient feeling of the human heart—that knowledge is better than riches; and it is deeply and sacredly true.

—SIDNEY SMITH

Why accumulate when there is so much joy in giving?

—SHAKER EXPRESSION

Basket Case

The market in Tehuacan was bustling. As I edged through the early crowd, I was taken by a lovely basket passing on a woman's back. It was heavily loaded, and she was small and old. Her hands held the tumpline at her temples to steady the load and to ease the strain.

I had been studying the crafts of Mexico for several years and was immediately taken by the beauty of this basket, which was more finely woven than any I had seen. Made of palm fibers, it was strong in a leathery way, with a subtle pattern worked into the weave that made you look twice to be sure it was really there.

Of course I followed the woman. She had arrived late at the market and was hurrying to get to her spot and begin selling her olives. When she was settled on her *petate*, kneeling with the basket of olives before her, I approached and tried to engage her in conversation. What followed was the strangest, most perplexing time I have ever had with a Mexican vendor. Usually they are affable, look you in the eye, and are extremely well at ease. On the contrary, this ancient one was shy, would not look directly at me, and spoke in monosyllables. Although frustrating, the situation was a challenge, and I was thoroughly enjoying myself.

Several times that morning, I returned to continue the "conversation." This basket was just too beautifully made to give up on. I *had* to locate the source. The ladies on the neighboring mats were also thoroughly enjoying the show.

They laughed and joshed this woman, who was old enough to be my mother's grandmother, about her new boyfriend, making her more (if possible) uncooperative than ever.

"Did you make your basket?"

"No."

"Will you sell it to me?"

"No."

"Why not? I'll pay you a good price."

She ignored me. Then she offered, "If I sell it to you, I'll have nothing to put my olives in."

"I'll buy you another basket and pay you for yours as well, so you can buy a nice new one when you get home."

"No!"

I offered to buy all of her olives (though I hate olives).

"No!"

"But why?"

"If I sell you my olives I will have nothing to do all day." (The neighbors were howling with delight.)

Finally we agreed upon a plan. She would sit all day and sell her olives. I would return at 5 P.M. and buy her remaining olives and her basket. By this time I learned that she as well as the lovely basket came from the village of Chilac—a bit lower down in the hot country than Tehuacan—where this special palm grew for weaving the baskets.

By the day's end Doña Anna was relaxed and smiling. We had become friends.

Beware of activities that require new clothes.

—Henry David Thoreau

friendships and love the finest decorations a home can have?

Simplicity in design and furnishings is a beautiful backdrop for human warmth.

On the other hand, fashion is a device to separate fools from their money, a snare to enrich merchants and producers. Do we need so much decoration in our lives? Can the world afford the expense?

Rather than be a follower of expensive fashions, why not be a leader in simple fashion? Be clothed in purpose, clarity, and kindness, and dress in a way that makes the best use of the world's supply of materials. Thoreau admonished us to "know your own bone." I would like to extend that to "wear your own clothes." If they are of your own make and design, so much the better, but whether or not you make them yourself, wear the clothes you like best, those that have a special meaning. If all of us would do this, we would feel freer, we would walk more easily.

How much richer the visual atmosphere would be if we abolished the fashion of luxury and replaced it with the comfort and rich variety of modern expressions of folk clothing and furnishings.

Among our finest treasures are jewels of the mind—the potential to discover the myriad facets and depths of truth, whether in philosophy, husbandry, or design. These are true treasures, with rewards that are ever growing, enriching both individuals and society, encouraging each being to develop to fullest potential.

Coveting or Sharing?

Hoarding is generally viewed as a sickness, a result of insecurity, and an expression of insensitivity to the needs of our fellows. How many of us are willing to face the fact that as a nation we are taking for our own use what rightfully belongs to others? As Americans we are generally

A poor woman, having covered her children with all the rags and bits of cloth and carpet she could find, was accustomed to lay down over all an old door which had come off its hinges. "Ah, mother," said the eldest daughter, "How I pity the poor children who haven't got a door to cover them."

—Ralph Waldo Emerson

proud of defending "liberty and justice for all." But unless we see this "all" as including all the other people of the world, that becomes a narrow partisan slogan upholding an oppressive privileged class not very different from that which many of our ancestors sought to escape in earlier times in other countries.

If we would each resolve to own no more than we ourselves can use and care for—be it land, clothes, tools, or toys—wealth would be more equitably distributed. If we need to hire someone else to care for our things, we own too much.

Some would argue that asking people to go without our accustomed luxuries would be a limitation on our freedom. But imagine eating only those foods that need few dishes to prepare and serve, instead of dining in a way that requires much more work for ourselves and others. The luxurious meal is not freedom at all, but the reverse. A simple meal can be most beautiful.

Simplicity is not just a personal, subjective approach to living, merely another fashion. Simplicity has long been recognized as a necessity by those aspiring to reach a higher plane of existence.

Violence is rooted in insecurity and want, and simplicity in living addresses both of these ills. By becoming involved in the shaping of things around us, we grow in self-confidence and knowledge with a resulting growth in security. By needing less ourselves, we make more of the world's store available to those in want. Covetousness is reduced when we have simple things that others can easily obtain for themselves.

The simpler something is to make, the more easily it can be replaced and the less we are dependent on special skills, materials, or markets. So simplicity is not just a matter of doing more with less, or spending less, or using less of the world's resources; it is a matter of freedom.

Until there are enough of the basics of life to go all the way around, it seems to me that we have an obligation to use our time, knowledge, and resources in ways that promote human growth. Giving a family a loaf of bread feeds them now, one time. Teaching them to raise wheat on land of their own feeds them permanently and makes them more self-respecting and self-sufficient. One gift beggars, the other builds a basis for a strong society.

WEALTH WITHOUT POVERTY

The condemning factor in the traditional definition of wealth was that there could be no riches without poverty. Like the two sides of a coin, one was necessary to have the other. The rich needed the poor for contrast, as a foundation for status, and to do their work. This is an explosive definition of wealth, containing within it violence and warfare.

It is crucial that we begin defining as wealth only those possessions and activities that do not make another poorer, that diminish no one. To build a society in which all are free to develop to their fullest, we must learn to enjoy the satisfactions of shared accomplishment,

---

Simplify your needs to the point where you can easily satisfy them yourself, so that those who live for the spirit do not add to the burdens of other men, taking away from them perhaps the very desire to develop the spiritual life also. What will it benefit if, in developing your spiritual life, you add to the burden of others and if in rising you oblige someone to descend correspondingly in the opposite direction. You will simply have increased a state of inequality and injustice.

—PIERRE CERESOLE

The Cost of a Home

The home you invest your time, energy, and money in should be one you prefer aesthetically—one you feel happy in. Only if the beauty of a curvilinear design excites you would I recommend building a yurt. The really big savings in these designs do not result from the elimination of rafters and corners, but from doing the design and construction work yourselves and from selecting materials that will be attractive when left exposed and finished simply with wax or oil. A paint-free exterior saves money and labor as well as future costs, including all the scraping to which you chain yourself as soon as you slap on that first dramatic coat of paint.

W. Coperthwaite

The approach of using low-maintenance materials can, of course, be applied to many other types of house besides a yurt, which reinforces my advice that the choice of a radically different form of structure to live in should be made from an aesthetic position—the feeling of pleasure you gain, living in the space—rather than just counting dollars saved during construction.

The design for a Family Yurt was developed to meet the needs of those who wanted a larger building than the Concentric Yurt. This design consists of a concentric yurt raised one story with another ring built around it, 53 feet in diameter, with a combined area of 2,700 square feet. My goal was to design this structure so that it could be built in stages to allow a family to start out with a very limited outlay of money, time, and energy, then expand the building as their resources grew. I aimed at an initial budget of $3,000. This figure would permit many people to bypass a mortgage, avoiding the usurious rates of the money lenders as well as their veto power over the design and time frame, with accompanying coercion to build a more expensive building than needed. As the stages of the larger design became more clearly defined, it evolved that the 16-foot-diameter central chamber could be begun with only $1,500 (in 1989) in cash. This central "hat box" of a room can be lived in until resources become available.

The second stage involves building a concentric yurt on top of and around the original room. The third stage is the construction of a large, sheltering roof spanning the outer ring. By putting layers of crushed stone underneath as a base, this area can serve as a porch, a garage, or a work and play area, and then, as additional rooms are needed, the outer ring can be enclosed with walls and floors.

There are many pressures on us to have our houses completed by the time we move in. The economic costs of this, as well as the resulting stresses in personal and family life, are tremendous. Why not take several years—or a lifetime—to create your home? Many of our most beautiful old houses were constructed over decades of building, and in the case of most farmsteads, over generations. Maybe we can learn an important lesson in this regard from the wisdom of our ancestors: an Asian proverb observes that a man is dead the day his house is finished.

wherein *we* gain pleasure from what *we* achieve, rather than *I*.

As we become more sensitive to that social body of which we're a part, we can plainly see that our neighbors' lack is our own impoverishment.

Louisa May Alcott grew up in a household with few material goods to spare; her mother took in washing to make ends meet. Yet looking back to her childhood she remarked, "I thought we were rich, as we were always giving to the poor." What a wonderful atmosphere for a child to grow in!

A wise, mature, and happy populace is our greatest natural resource. Each of the world's children that dies prematurely—from illness, malnutrition, violence, or neglect—is a precious treasure lost from the world's store. Even the most shortsighted and callous of us must realize that we need all the wisdom and talent we can muster if we are to solve the problems facing the world, and that it is stupid and dangerous to have malnourished, unhappy, stunted people as neighbors.

> While the world hungers for knowledge of
> how to build, raise food, and effectively organize
> society, we turn our mature minds out to graze:
> to retirement. In many fields the years from sixty on
> are the richest in skill, perspective, concern,
> and wisdom.
> We are shocked by a businessman who wastes capital
> or a farmer who lets topsoil wash away; why are we
> less concerned with the waste of our human capital,
> our most valuable resource?

Not Losing but Winning

We are accustomed to thinking in game terms, of winning and losing. We need to develop a philosophy of life in which there are no losers, a world where everyone can win.

Wealth can help us to do what we want, or help us to develop more fully. But often what is more valuable than financial power is an ability to recognize what is relatively most important. For instance, to me, a shower is an important adjunct to creative thinking, on par with a library. Likewise, finding just the right axe or hoe can be so essential to some people that they spend a good deal of effort in finding the one that suits them. This can be as satisfying as seeking out the latest style of car, yet costs the world much less.

"Success" is an increase in well-being, and "wealth" is the acquiring of creative, productive ability. In the past, success has generally been relative and competitive—measured by the failure of others. It now behooves us to think in terms of cooperative success, wherein we feel happy as the group about us succeeds. After all, what does it gain us to be "successful" in a failing society or, as J. Goldsmith has said, "To win in a poker game on the Titanic"?

I reckon—when I count at all—
First—Poets—Then the Sun
Then Summer—Then the Heaven of God
And then—the list is done—

But Looking back—the First so seems
To Comprehend the Whole—
The Others look a needless Show—
So I write—Poets—All

—Emily Dickinson

85

A Democratic Chair

W. Coperthwaite

Is there such a thing as democratic furniture? If so, what would a democratic chair look like?

Most of the fine chairs we see today, if handmade, take nearly as much skill as boat building and, if made with power tools, require much investment in equipment and acquiring the skills needed. I would like to see what those who are reading this might come up with for ideas for a handmade chair that is light, comfortable, strong, beautiful, simple to make from easily found materials. (All we seek is perfection.)

Utopian? Or impossible, to create an egalitarian chair? Not at all. As a society we have simply not yet focused on this problem. When we do, there will be some elegant chairs as a result (or boats … or houses … or wheelbarrows … (not necessarily in combination—although, come to think of it, there have been some very comfortable wheelbarrows, some very fine houseboats, and several wheelbarrow boats.…)

My suggestion for the most democratic chair follows. This is not provided to represent an ideal but in hopes of stimulating even better designs from you, the readers.

To Make the Democratic Chair:

1. Saw and whittle out the four pieces shown in diagram, using white pine 7/8-inch thick.

2. Bevel the front edges of the two base pieces to meet at the angle shown, then nail together.

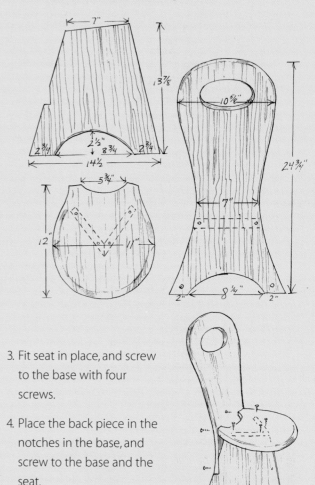

3. Fit seat in place, and screw to the base with four screws.

4. Place the back piece in the notches in the base, and screw to the base and the seat.

86

I have done without electricity and tend the fireplace and stove myself. Evenings I light the old lamps. There is no running water and I pump water from the well. I chop the wood and cook the food. These simple acts make man simple; and how difficult it is to be simple.

—CARL JUNG

SIMPLICITY

To some people, mention of simplicity suggests the crude, the drab, and the ugly—a gray or khaki-colored world of unlimited bleakness. Yet for me the word "simplicity" is rich with melody—my feet want to "skip to flutes." This is a word that glows in yellows and reds like autumn leaves, suggesting elegance—physical, moral, philosophical, and aesthetic elegance.

So, count me not with the disenchanted but among the enchanted: enchanted with the possibilities for a life of simplicity and beauty for *all* people, everywhere.

I am amazed at the beauty of fire and equally so with the workings of a watch or a piece of music. The human skill that has produced them is wondrous. There is great beauty in learning to go light, to do with as little as possible, to shed the superfluous, and to carry so little baggage in life that you need no porter. There is a special richness in seeking to live in a way that is open to all, in being part of a movement to share the world's riches fairly, and to feel that no one need suffer because of the way you live.

Going light can be simply elegant. A simple meal can be more satisfying than a banquet.

SIMPLICITY AND DESIGN

If we intend to design a society where the needs of all can be met, this will necessarily mean learning to live simply.

We need to design a way to live gently on this earth, borrowing what we need from nature's storehouse with tenderness, care, and thanksgiving, grateful for the privilege of dwelling here awhile. If we take more than we need for our sustenance, we thieve from those who have not enough.

We need to design technologies—gentle, thoughtful technologies—and we have the wisdom of many people to draw upon. The need for new perspectives is so urgent that we can ill afford to neglect any source of wisdom wherever it can be found, be it ancient or modern, nomadic or sedentary, rural or urban. We need a blending of the best we can find to create technologies customfitted to human needs and ecology, because another urgent need is to learn to live more lightly on the earth.

Live simply—that others may simply live.

—ELIZABETH SETON

To require little is better capital than to earn much. The need to earn much enslaves a man, while the ability to do with little makes him free. He who needs little will more easily strive toward the goals he has in view, and will in general lead a richer, fuller life than he who has many wants.

—FRIDTJOF NANSEN

The yurt design shown in the photograph at the beginning of this chapter is a symbol of such blending. The basic concept of the structure has been borrowed from ancient nomads living on the steppes of central Asia, who untold centuries ago found that they could increase the space in their circular tents by raising them on a low wall, providing support by tying a rope about them. The structure, made of light poles fastened with rawhide, then covered with felt and bound together with bands of woven wool, was a brilliant solution to the needs of that harsh region's people.

Out of admiration for the technical genius of these people, the word "yurt" is used in the name of the Yurt Foundation. The modern yurt combines the sheltering and design skills of nomadic herdsmen with modern materials (steel cable, glass, lumber) suited for use in another time and climate. The resulting new structure is not better, only different, designed to meet different needs. A Mongolian yurt in Maine would be terribly expensive (have you priced wool felt in Madawaska lately?) and would likely collapse under the first heavy rain. A modern yurt in Mongolia would be equally ridiculous (have you priced white pine and cedar shingles in Ulan Bator lately?), and its weight would make it impractical for moving about with the herds.

Yet it would be extremely difficult to improve upon the traditional structure, even with all our collected knowledge to draw upon, *if we were to use only the materials available to the nomads.* This recognition highlights for me the genius, skill, and sensitivity to design embedded in folk cultures. We tend to compare airplanes to Eskimo kayaks and draw very biased conclusions concerning our own superiority. But if we were to put a Thomas Edison ashore on the coast of Greenland and ask him to build a superior kayak *using only local materials,* it

The professionals guard their language jealously to make themselves indispensable.

—Christopher Alexander

is questionable whether he could build a better boat than the Eskimos have done since time immemorial. Even let him have a skilled traditional kayak builder to help. (I would give an eye tooth or two to be on the beach watching those wise old guys building that kayak.)

This is not meant to say that native wisdom cannot be improved upon. We should try to improve technique whenever we can, but let us do so with humility, with respect for those who have gone before and shown us the way.

The human mind has vast potential. I believe that with our minds we can muster the ability to design a culture to fit human needs.

Choosing Technologies

What kind of technology do we need? This is a relatively unprecedented question. Prior to the industrial revolution, societies did not consciously select a technology to fit its people's needs but rather made use of whatever happened along. If an invention was new, it was usually considered better. The flush toilet was considered to be an advance over the privy; the mechanical dishwasher, an improvement over doing dishes by hand; the chain saw, better than the axe.

More and more people are now questioning this uncritical enthusiasm for whatever is new. Cutting wood by hand may be considered old-fashioned, yet if you study axe and saw types and select the best from around the

W. Coperthwaite

The axe is a symbol. Each person's situation and needs are different, and those who live in the desert or prairies may find it hard to get as carried away by an axe as I do. Yet each of us needs to think through our daily activities and see if we are living the life we enjoy and can defend ethically and intellectually to ourselves. If we would all endeavor to do so, we could build a new culture: happier, gentler, simpler, and more beautiful.

world, the efficiency derived from this knowledge is new—new knowledge is new technology.

The chain saw, on the other hand, is an example of a modern industrial tool adversely affecting the overall design of our lives. As a production tool, intended for cutting a great deal of wood in a short time, the motorized saw is astounding. Yet we make a common error when we assume that a production tool or process is best for home use. Many reason that the chain saw is an advance in wood cutting for all situations. As a result, many people now own chain saws, despite their danger, air and noise pollution, and high cost, for casual home use.

While when cutting pulpwood it would be ridiculous to compete against a power saw with a bow saw and axe, home-scale firewood harvesting is another story. It takes less than five minutes per day to cut my whole year's supply of wood (3 cords) using a bow saw and an axe, and doing the hauling by wheelbarrow. This is both exercise and recreation. I take great pleasure in being able to heat my home without the noise and smell of a power saw. There is much less danger and no need for fossil fuel.

The point being that a chain saw is not a better tool than an axe, only different. Both tools are useful, but with different areas of efficiency.

Although these days they are in fashion, power tools are greatly overrated for home use. Many people buy them thinking that they will be more efficient than hand tools, others for the macho effect—power and noise. Some people have simply never learned the hand skills needed and therefore rely on that extra power to bull through a job.

And yet, what a marvelously simple tool the axe is, with no dependency on the factory for parts and lasting many lifetimes. It is quiet, easily carried, and doesn't smoke. There is enormous satisfaction in using an axe—

the same one year after year—realizing that its development reaches back to before the dawn of history. A very basic tool, which our ancestors designed well, works as beautifully today as it ever did. The feeling of kinship with the ancients that this continuity brings is deeply satisfying. We need as many of these bridges to the past as we can discover.

> Many people have sought the simple life
> not from necessity but for the very beauty
> of this way of living and the sense it brings
> of closeness to the world around us.

RELIGIONS AND MORALS

Buddhism teaches nonattachment to things. This thinking may have evolved due to scarcity and was meant as an aid to rid us of the problems of coveting and all that feeling's accompanying unhappiness.

But is attachment good or evil? And attachment to what—to things? to people? to places? Is it possible that Buddhism's nonattachment to things developed as an expedient, as an escape, as a response to a violent society, rather than as a good way to live in itself? If we choose to redesign our society and place the highest value on simple things, self-made, available to all, would not nonattachment lose its necessity?

Here is a question that holds the potential to alter our perception of religion. Instead of asking of a particular faith, "What is its wisdom?" ask "How did this set of beliefs come about, and why? What were the social conditions that produced this religion?"

Many of the great religions arose in conditions of terrible poverty, suffering, and violence. They were bounded by the technological level of their time, as well as by the surrounding social structure, often tyranny. Given that history, is it possible the products of the material world were put down because they were seen as unattainable?

If this sounds like taking on Gautama, Jesus, and Gandhi all at once, it is. With all due respect to those gentle sages, I believe that they can be wrong. I also believe that they would encourage us to seek out the weaknesses in their teachings. Herein lies their strength, in that they can be questioned and stand the test. And most of the time their ways are found to be valid—but not always. Their errors may be very small, but unless we allow for the possibility of error we are no better than the blind followers of a Hitler or a Peter the Hermit. We have nothing to fear and much to gain from a respectful doubting. What we need to be wary of, if we are to build a better society, is the blind following of leaders, teachers, or gurus. We do not need to fear questioning.

> Descartes doubted, questioned, all things
> in order that he might know.

When man began to desire private property, then entered violence, fraud, theft, and rapine. Soon after, pride and envy broke out in the world and brought with them a new standard of wealth for men, who, until then, thought themselves rich when they wanted nothing, now rated their demands not by the calls of nature, but by the plenty of others, and began to consider themselves poor when they beheld their own possessions exceeded by those of others.

—SAMUEL JOHNSON

THINGS

What if we've been wrong about things? What if there is nothing wrong with wanting and having things? That is, what's been wrong has been our relationship to things, all our coveting, greed, and lust for ownership. What would be wrong with possessions if they deprived no one? If they were made by oneself or by friends and were not for sale but freely and lovingly given?

If we sought only simple things—things that cost little, or that could be made and owned by nearly everyone—there would be no need to covet, and things could be raised to their proper level of respect and equality.

In the process we would learn more about simplicity.

Things *have had a bad rap.*
For millennia we've been asked to
Abjure things
As the root of much evil—
Greed—covetousness—jealousy—
Theft—war.
If we would not strive to own things,
The world would be a happier place, say the sages.
But: what if
Our attitude toward things changed.
What if they could not be bought but only given?
In a society that appreciated a thing
Because a friend had made it,
The object given might be burned or lost or broken
But the finest part of the gift would remain.
If all wanted to have this feeling
There would be no value in buying or stealing,
But only in freely giving.

Once the emphasis has been placed on possessing a skill rather than an object, we are in a realm of creative wealth that is free to all who seek it.

When there is plenty, and when our focus is on making rather than on having, things can be a source of pleasure and satisfaction. Moreover, designing to fit this criterion is a delight.

To meet that criteria, things need to be:

— low in cost
— simple to make and easily replaced
— easily cared for
— pleasing to the eye and the mind
— not dangerous to use, make, or dispose of
— durable, aging well (as does glass, wood, cotton, leather, copper, and ceramics)
— made with care and affection

SIMPLICITY AND FAIRNESS

Simple living is less violent and less exploitative. When we live in complexity, our needs are so great in terms of energy and material goods that we live at the expense of others. As we simplify our homes, our clothes, and our eating habits, not only is less work needed to supply us but also less effort to maintain our way of life, as well.

As the people of the world who are now exploited begin to get a fair return for their labor, prices will rise. We must expect this and be willing to pay the costs, otherwise we are hypocrites of the first water, wanting the world's people to be well off yet still insisting that our bananas be cheap. When the people picking the bananas in Honduras, tapping the rubber trees in Malaya, mining tin in Bolivia, and making shoes in Brazil get the same return for their labor that we do, our bananas and boots and tires and tin will cost more.

Learning to live simply enables us to do our share of the world's work. I have no right to have more than I can produce. If I take economic advantage of others—whether through the economic position of my country, my inherited wealth, or my inherited intelligence and muscle, filling my house with luxury—I thieve.

In Emerson's sense of the need for "leaving the world a bit better" than we found it, shouldn't we look at what we consume of the world's wealth and make sure that we contribute in proportion to what we use?

As I've said before: it seems woefully inconsistent to use electricity to pump water and then jog for exercise. Pumping water by hand is no great chore, and when we get our water this way, we tend to be more conscious of the amount we are using. A family nearby here in Maine has their pump connected to a bicycle.

There is a tendency in our "civilization" to look on those who live without running water or electricity as backward. But if we were to face the facts of our actual impacts on the world around us, doesn't it seem more backward to play golf for bodily exercise while consuming fossil fuels to drive to the local grocery store?

As we become more sensitive to ways in which our lives can become integrated with our beliefs, such tasks as pumping water and splitting wood may come to be recognized as truly beautiful parts of life. There is enormous beauty in being able to do with as little as possible: going light, doing more with less. The opinion of the revered General Forrest (who said, "We got thar the fustest with the mostest . . .") to the contrary, I'm interested in getting there lastest with the leastest.

> When we have more than we need while others
> are in want, we certainly thieve. But in addition,
> we enslave ourselves. As we learn to live with
> fewer and simpler things, and are able to live with fewer
> expenses, we become less vulnerable
> to social upheaval. We have greater freedom—
> visual, mental, and spatial—and far greater freedom
> of movement. And we spend less time maintaining and
> stumbling over things—physically, mentally,
> and visually—and worrying about loss.

CHOICES AND BALANCES

Some people would be surprised to learn that I use paper towels. Yet when people object to "using all those trees," they usually fail to acknowledge the trees that go into their daily newspaper. Each of us must make our own choices, hopefully thoughtful ones. At this stage in my development, I find paper towels to be useful. I use them in small quantities, cutting each roll in half to give a more convenient size with less waste (which also halves my sin, *n'est pas?*). This saves me the energy required to launder cloth towels, which in my case, living far from town and

---

To laugh often and to love much, to win the respect of intelligent persons and the affection of children; to earn the approbation of honest critics and endure the betrayal of false friends; to appreciate beauty; to find the best in others; to give oneself; to leave the world a bit better whether by a healthy child, a garden patch or a redeemed social condition; to have played and laughed with enthusiasm and sung with exultation; to know even one life has breathed easier because you have lived; this is to have succeeded.

—RALPH WALDO EMERSON

the power line, would be more costly, economically and ecologically. Someday I may grow to live without the particular convenience of paper towels, but they seem to me to be all right for now.

Here's another example of making a simpler choice. If you want to remove pitch, tar, or engine grease from your hands, any clean vegetable oil will do. A dab of margarine or salad oil is all that is needed. Rub it in well, wipe off the residue, then wash with warm water and soap. For stubborn tar, repeat the process, which works like magic and is kinder to the hands than the kerosene, gasoline, or paint thinner that is often used.

We are much concerned today with the misuse of natural resources, of air and water pollution. But how about inner pollution? Are we not a part of the environment too? A special kind of life that needs care? Yet we carelessly feed our bodies poisons in the form of food additives, junk food, and drugs, legal and illegal. Junk food is not only directly harmful for the body but also has to be manufactured, packaged, and transported, all of which waste energy and materials.

We also pollute our minds and stifle our creativity with a clutter of things, words, ideas—distractions and stimulants. This clutter blinds us—impoverishes—conceals beauty—and steals time and energy from growth and vitality. How beautiful it would be to learn to treat our bodies as carefully as we treat our temples, entering in stocking feet and in quietness . . . to treat our spirits like gardens we water and care for and encourage to grow.

Each of us has only a small amount to invest in the building of a better world—our self. This may be small, but it is all we have. How we care for that self and how we bestow our energies is of the highest importance, in terms of what we do directly and what we do indirectly by example or by joining with kindred spirits. Waste of our self is a violation of the first order. How can we be truly sensitive to the spirit of another if we are not first aware of our own essence?

Our present society is based to a dangerous extent on exploitation, on taking advantage of one another. Most stores, for instance, are run to make a profit from the customers rather than to help supply people's needs. This does not need to be so. Our way of living and of doing business must change fundamentally if a valid cultural design is to emerge. We must learn to run stores because we enjoy this way of contributing to a community's well-being, helping customers find the highest-quality products for their needs.

It is often assumed that the chief reason for making things—furniture, clothing, toys, a garden— is to save money. There are other factors that may be of equal or greater importance: making what we need for life is a way of expressing creativity and of gaining greater confidence. Emotional security comes from providing the necessities of life in personal, meaningful ways, by our own hands or those of friends and loved ones. Another value in studying how things are made is to increase our appreciation for them as we better understand what makes them work. The knowledge that comes from shaping the things around us helps us build relationships with the world that are more intimate.

HANDS

Our understanding would be enlarged immensely if we were all to become artisans in some manner, fairly competent at a certain craft. How else can we raise in esteem and value those who do hand work to the level of those

It would be well if we were all good hand-craftsmen in some craft and the dishonor of manual labor done away with.

—John Ruskin

If I buy one necessity of life—
I cheat myself to some extent.

—Henry David Thoreau

Stephen Lanzalotta, master carver.

who sell, study, photograph—those who enjoy a crafter's fine work but fail to respect the person who makes beautiful things by hand?

The world over, people love fine baskets but grant low status to the basket maker. Panama hats are much sought after, but the hat maker is among the worst paid. Fine shoes are admired, but not the shoemaker.

We perpetuate these injustices by the way we live. We can become more sensitive and can increase respect for all walks of life by personally experiencing as many of these walks as we can. If all of us learned to work with our hands, all of us would have more respect for others who work with their hands.

When as a society we fail to help all people have confidence in their ability to create, we are doubly wasteful. First, we lose from society's reservoir the creative potential of so many, and second, we see those who are left out lose wellbeing and emotional security. The price in individual frustration and its attendant ills is too high.

If, on the ground floor of life, all people were encouraged to develop the use of their hands fully, as a society we would experience an ever growing enrichment in the design and quality of the things surrounding us, as everyone gained a tactile relationship with materials and techniques.

Another benefit of experience with artisanal crafts is a blending of the work of head and hands—each day if possible, and ideally in the same activity.

An educator in whom this basic wisdom was apparent was Morris Mitchell. He directed the Putney Graduate School of Education in the mid-1950s. A master at blending the physical and intellectual in daily life, he liked to garden, to build stone walls, and to make furniture. On one side of his office sat a large handsome desk that had been his father's before him, and on the other stood a

A Rain Barrel

Rain barrels are nice to have on a homestead. Here at home, free soft water flows off the cedar-shingled roof. But wooden barrels are getting harder to find, and those made of plastic or steel just do not feel right.

Why not make one yourself? Cooper it. Yes, but … that takes a high level of skill, and I'm seeking ways to work that need less skill and less equipment than coopering requires.

A hollow log seemed like a promising solution, and a hollow *cedar* log would be even better. In this region, white cedar abounds. Often the trunks are hollow-hearted, easing the job of making a container from one. But to find a cedar that is not split, large enough for a barrel (24 inches in diameter), takes some searching. I put the word out to several people who work in the woods, but to no avail. Two years passed and still no cedar-log rain barrel.

While tramping about in a cedar swamp looking for moose tracks one winter day, I came upon a huge cedar stump about eight feet high. I began to salivate (mentally). This was too good to be true—a big, dead, hollow piece of cedar trunk, on my own land, and not a quarter mile from home. Closer inspection proved the remaining wood to be sound.

This was a job for two. A friend offered to help and I readied the tools. The appointed day came—and no friend. Eager to work on the barrel, I pondered the possibilities of handling the job alone. It is my suspicion that "necessity is the mother of invention" was first voiced in regard to homesteading. Many times there are no extra hands available and a way has to be found to do a job on your own.

As a youngster, I learned to handle a two-man crosscut saw alone, but for cutting up felled trees, not for cutting them down. By removing the handle on the off side, and by keeping the blade vertical, I found that one could saw alone.

This worked well. The chief disadvantage, compared with a one-person bow saw, was that due to its thicker blade the crosscut saw cut a wider kerf in the log, thus using more energy.

But the extra challenge this time was to cut down a standing tree, with a horizontal cut—alone. The sagging end of the saw, normally supported by the other sawyer, seemed likely to take all the fun out of the job.

Over the next day or two, several schemes came to mind. One was to hang the off end of the saw from a pivoting pair of shears that would move back and forth with the motion of the saw. This would have worked, but a better method appeared.

I made a small platform on the off side of the tree, and on this nailed waxed oak lathes, on which to slide the other end of the saw. This worked like a charm. When I had sawed the tree down, I cut it to length and found it to be massively heavy. There was a 6-inch hole in the center, surrounded by much frozen wood. I would have to work it down to size there in the woods until it was light enough to carry. Here was another challenge.

The hole in the center was too small for an axe or an adze. A slick (a large boat-building chisel) bit in at the corners and was frustrating. A big, gouge-shaped slick would have helped, but none was at hand. After scratching away at the problem (both physically and mentally), an idea came for a new tool for this job: a long gougelike tool heavy enough to permit hard thrusting.

In the tool box there was an old gutter adze that I'd found in Hungary. I bolted this onto a shovel handle, gouge fashion. After putting a good edge on the blade, it worked beautifully, either when thrusting or using in a chopping motion, like cutting a hole in the ice of a frozen pond. A week of chopping away at odd moments produced a fine cedar barrel: 1 inch thick, 24 inches in diameter, light enough to be carried home on a shoulder.

By the way, I also found the moose tracks I'd been looking for, as well as the moose—a mother and a new calf.

work bench. He would alternate as the day went on, at one moment writing a letter and the next fitting an arm to a chair. Here was a delightful mixture of ink and shavings.

Gandhi too believed in blending the labor of head and hands. He found physical work an aid to contemplation.

PRODUCTION

I remember as a student hearing the statement that "we have solved the problems of production," evidently meaning that we knew how to produce the quantity of products that the world needs and that the unsolved problem was distribution.

I now believe there is an underlying fallacy in that thinking. Yes, distributing knowledge and other types of resources fairly is an urgent need. But the assumption that industrial production solves the world's problems is an error with far-reaching effects. *How* we produce is at least as important as *what* we produce. Until the emotional and educational components are considered as important factors, we have not solved the problem of production.

A modern tire plant may seem very efficient in the way it converts raw materials into a usable product, but it may be terribly inefficient in the deadening effects it has on the people who spend their working life pulling tires from molds. There are enormous costs, to individuals and to society, in investing lives in such repetitive, noxious. and mentally dulling activity.

Perhaps a better example of the inefficiency in human terms of industrial production is in the spinning and knitting of wool. Compared to hand methods, the *quantity* of material that machines can produce is incredible. As for quantity of material turned out in a given time, competition between machines and hand knitters would be ridiculous. And yet, hand knitting is one of the most efficient methods of production ever developed, *when all costs are considered.* "He's mad!" you say, but read on.

— The outlay for hand tools is very small, while the cost of production machinery is a gigantic investment. This allows the tools of hand knitting to be available to all, making knitting a genuinely democratic craft.
— The hand work is portable. It can be done on the train or while visiting friends. The knitter is not tied to a specific workplace.
— Knitting is quiet work and does not interfere with conversation. Its soothing repetitive action does not interfere with thought.
— Knitting can be done at odd moments in the day when the hands are idle and desiring activity.

Knitting is an extremely ancient craft that remains altogether viable today. This quality of timelessness adds to the knitting's incomparable, unquantifiable beauty. There are many old techniques of hand work still alive and well—including felt making (for boots, rugs, and hats); leather work (for clothing and implements); wood carving (for spoons, bowls, and paddles)—but knitting is the finest of them all. (How is that for a bald, unadulterated, first-class prejudice?)

DESIGNING SIMPLICITY

Design in its best sense means analyzing a problem and seeking the best solution. In order for more people to share in the joy of shaping the things they use, designs need simplifying in all fields. There is greater beauty in simpler forms and greater efficiency in saving materials, time, and energy.

The important role of design in education has so often been ignored. Likewise, for too long the crafts have had an aura of the unattainable. This appears to function as a sort of psychological protective tariff for the members of an exclusive club. Frequently, emphasis is put on the most difficult designs rather than the simplest. This is another example of a wasteful approach to life, preserving an aristocracy of the initiated and treating talent as something you either have or don't have.

But talent is continuum. Everyone has some talent, large or small. For me, an important measure of a civilization's success is how fully it develops the talents of all its people. We need this development both for an individual's own sake and for the enrichment of society at large. The pool of talent is one of our world's richest resources.

A design goal of mine has been to create forms that the least skilled and least confident could make successfully—beautiful, simple, and useful designs, truly democratic designs that will invite people to use their hands.

House-raising works well as a situation for exploring

From the Sufi tradition I came to see that the artisan was meant to transform himself through his work. While striving to transmute the materials' physical limitations, the artisan was striving to transform his own soul.

—NARER ARDELAN

these questions, because the size of such a project engenders growth in the participants' self-confidence. Also, there seems to be a deep-seated respect in most of us for shelter and the ability to shape it.

The complexity of various crafts has been well explored and is in no need of discussion. But the challenges of fostering simplicity, with the purpose of making crafts available to all, as their right—these have been neglected.

For too long the various fields of knowledge have been closed to the majority of people, because of knowledge barriers (such as entrance exams), financial barriers (tuition), class barriers (guilds, unions, and directors of admission), language barriers (each group adopting its own arcane terminology with the supposed purpose of facilitating communication among members but with the effect of being a rebuff to the uninitiated). These obstacles are undemocratic in that they do not let an individual have free access to the knowledge that society has collected—our common inheritance, the greatest store of wealth to which we are all heirs.

Such barriers have resulted in an elite group that understands and a mass of outsiders who are excluded from knowledge. For example, in earlier times the Bible was only available in Latin or Greek and accessible exclusively to priests and scholars. That exclusivity is kept alive today in the medical profession.

There are innumerable, hidden psychological and social pressures that keep people from being free to explore the constructive use of their hands and minds. Because of artificial limitations on who shall know, society fails to reap the knowledge, the productivity, and the peace and well-being that come from universal participation. In a very real sense, we are hoarding our wealth rather than investing it in the best blue chip stock on the market— human ability.

BUILDING CONFIDENCE

Certain objects and materials have more appeal than others. If a form of work is to give confidence and a sense of purpose to the uninitiated, it must not only be simple and attractive, it must also have a certain magical quality.

Boats have this quality, as do structures such as tree houses, log cabins, tipis, yurts. The projects that seem to work best are those done from clear-cut patterns, forms that require little in the way of complicated designing on the part of the maker. The creative challenges will come later, once basic skills have been learned.

Initially what is important is to be able to successfully make a useful object over which the maker can exclaim, with pleasure and amazement, "I made this myself!"

This eliminates, as first projects, things that need to fit, for instance, shoes or sweaters; a sweater that fits poorly is defeating for a beginning knitter. Leather bags work well as learning projects, for they can be visually appealing, simple in design, and easy to construct. Belts are also good for starters.

My exploration of this learning process is still preliminary, and I would appreciate corresponding with others who are involved in similar searching.

I've seen how a canoe paddle can be a delightful first project in woodworking. There is mystery and beauty in a canoe paddle—in the experience of shaping it, something haunting and spirit-touching. Yet all that is needed is a sharp knife and a plank of spruce reasonably clear of knots (yellow cedar is especially nice if you can find some).

Simply whittle away the part you don't want. Almost any shape will do. Smoothness and a good feel in the hands are the chief criteria. Remember, you can paddle a canoe quite well with a board, and you are only trying to make the piece of wood lighter, smoother, better able to slip into the water. The most common mistake is thinning the shaft too much—avoid this, and your paddle is bound to work.

Talk not to me of Summer Trees
The foliage of the mind
A Tabernacle is for Birds
Of no corporeal kind

—EMILY DICKINSON

TERRITORY

Defense of territory is a rather common response of people to what they perceive as threats to "their" land. Territory appears to be important not only for physical well-being (as with a home and food supply) but psychologically as well. We feel more secure when we can delineate a territory as our own

As long as there is territory enough for everyone to have a domain, peace is possible. But with the dwindling of space relative to population, the physical and psychological preconditions for violence increase. Limited resources have made people fight with one another in the past. Often the resources struggled over have not been for immediate use but to increase one group's status and respect in the eyes of others. Sometimes the prize has been land, sometimes money, at other times power and position.

Advocates of the settling (or unsettling?) of space would have no trouble in finding adequate "territory" for all. Yet we might find Tolstoy's story, "How Much Land Does a Man Need?" pertinent, wherein ultimately a man learns that he "needs" only a plot of ground, six feet of earth.

The late John Calhoun of the National Institute of Mental Health suggested a way in which without infringing on the needs of others everyone can have a territory

---

The present position which we, the educated and well-to-do classes, occupy, is that of the old man of the sea, riding on the poor man's back; only unlike the old man of the sea, we are very sorry for the poor man, very sorry; and we will do almost anything for the poor man's relief. We will not only supply him with food sufficient to keep him on his legs, but we will teach and instruct him and point out the beauties of the landscape: We will discourse sweet music to him and give him an abundance of good advice: Yes, we will do almost anything for the poor man, anything but get off his back.

—TOLSTOY

of their own. This is mental territory—intellectual territory. The world of thought, of design, of creativity is large enough for all. Calhoun believed that mental territory can have much the same psychological value as land, without the disadvantage of being limited. Each person can find an area of his or her own. The potential for exploration in the field of knowledge is so vast that all who seek an area of their own can find it. This view of territory also has the advantage that two can occupy the same space at the same time without interference.

This is truly a nonviolent concept of territory, especially meaningful to those of us who have not yet attained that state of enlightened selfishness in which we find our success in the success of others.

Exploration can also bring great satisfaction, without necessitating personal ownership of territory. To explore a piece of ocean, for instance, can be very rewarding. The traveler leaves no trail. While some find excitement in feeling that they are the first to be in a given spot, others find joy in discovering an old stone wall or cellar hole in the woods, knowing that fellow explorers tarried awhile at this place before.

Does territory need to be owned and defensible? Or can it be something we identify with? I wonder if there are not other ways of perceiving territory that can fill our needs to have an area we feel is our own. Perhaps we can satisfy that need by taking on a piece of work that needs

doing but which others have not gotten around to focusing on. For example, planting rugosa roses on exposed parts of a shore, to keep the land from being eroded by the sea. These roses hold the slope as well as provide a wonderful fruit.

There is an isolated spot in this part of Maine where three roads meet. Each year a family living nearby plants

Soto! Explore thyself!
Therein thyself shall find
The "Undiscovered Continent"—
No Settler had the Mind.

—EMILY DICKINSON

To live content with small means, to seek elegance rather than luxury, and refinement rather than fashion; to be worthy, not respectable, and wealthy not rich, to study hard, think quietly, talk gently, act frankly, to listen to the stars and birds, to babes and sages with an open heart; to bear all cheerfully, do all bravely, await occasions, hurry never, in a word, to let the spiritual, unbidden, grow up through the common.

—WILLIAM CHANNING

a flower garden in the triangle in the center, giving delight to all who pass.

One of the finest experiences is to discover interrelationships of thought that we did not previously recognize. To create, out of our own experience, new ideas, new solutions, is joy compounded. Exploration in the physical world is exciting but no less so in the world of the mind. We owe to all children the opportunity to grow up with a greater vision of their own inner potential.

Blake found the universe in a grain of sand. Thoreau suggests another approach to territory when he refers to having a greater claim to Concord than those with recorded deeds. His knowledge of the woods and fields made them *his* in a very special way, one that was not in conflict with the legal owners. Can we not find territories of our own such as Blake and Thoreau did: a river, a woodland, a library, a social condition?

There is a rural maxim that admonishes the farmer
to always come home with a stone in hand.
In this way, with each passing, the field is cleared
of one more stone while providing one more stone
for building. Here in the wilds of Maine, firewood
is stacked along the trail. On each return trip
it is easy to pick up a stick to carry home.
Everything we do either helps to build
a better world or hinders it.
We can choose to be either a part
of the solution or a part
of the problem.

The Neglected Shaving Horse

One of the most useful yet neglected tools from our ancestral warehouse is the humble shaving horse. A century ago it was more common than the bench vice. At that time this semiportable clamp was common on farm and homestead, as well as in shops of great variety, from shingle maker and cooper to bodger and ladder maker—its use with a drawknife results in an incredibly efficient partnership.

The shaving horse is ingenious in its simplicity of construction and operation—one of the unsung wonders of folk wisdom. Its basic elements are a plank seat with a clamp that is pivoted by the foot to hold the work while the two-handled drawknife is pulled along the work by the operator. Some ingenious mind in the dim past realized that depressing a pivoted arm with the foot could result in great clamping pressure at the top of the bench, freeing both hands to control the cutting edge and to give more power. As one pulls off a shaving, the effort applied by the hands forces one to brace with the feet, automatically gripping the work and holding it fast.

The advent of machinery and the factory system forced many potential handcrafters into becoming machine operators and exiled the shaving horse nearly into oblivion. Now the balance has begun to tip back, as more and more crafters are rediscovering the beauty of the shaving horse, which in the past two decades has continued to evolve, with new designs developing.

My fascination with shaving horses goes back some forty years, and I continue to marvel at their variety, from the ponderous and heavy to the delicate ones of the itinerant Italian chair makers who carry their shaving horses with them on their shoulders. They also vary from the crude to the elegant, from the ugly to the beautiful—from those that take hours to make to one that can be in operation an hour after commencing.

There are three basic types:

T. Gilmore

First, the "standard" shaving horse. It has a swingle tree that is open on three sides for clamping stock against the table piece.

Second is the bodger's shaving horse with an open swingle tree, which is better for holding wider stock but is somewhat less convenient for working long pieces. It is the simplest to make.

Third is the *panko di seggellaio* of the nomadic Italian chair maker.

The latter is an especially beautiful design—the Windsor chair of shaving horses. The demand for a light yet strong horse has resulted in economy of material and a simple yet efficient and lovely form. The work is not gripped by friction as in the first two designs, but is pressed by the swingle tree against a ledge on the central post, requiring very little pressure to hold the piece. Larger work can be accommodated by either tipping the swingle tree at a steeper angle or by moving the pivot farther away. It is the most specialized shaving horse, in that it is made to work best for chair posts and rungs. The following story describes my first encounter with a *panko di seggellaio*.

In the small French village of Haute Claire live three tapestry weavers. Their work is a delight to behold, adorning walls of museums, banks, and universities. Pat, Jaqueline, and Michelle, known as *Les Tisserandes*, met at the Ecole de Beaux Arts in the early 1960s, finding common purpose in their concern for peace, simple living, and vegetarianism. They wanted to live such a life themselves and to weave their values into their work, like the tapestry weavers of old. They found an abandoned priory and set to work restoring it. There, in the mid-1960s, I found a beautiful example of three people putting their philosophy into daily living.

While there, I saw the most interesting shaving horse I had yet seen. From Italy traveled itinerant chair makers, the *seggellaio*. They would come to your place, cut the needed wood from the hedgerow, and shave it into chair parts. After constructing and bottoming your chairs, they moved on.

The secret to efficient chair making by hand is a shaving horse. Normally shaving horses are quite heavy. But here was one as lightly made as the chairs shaved in it, truly

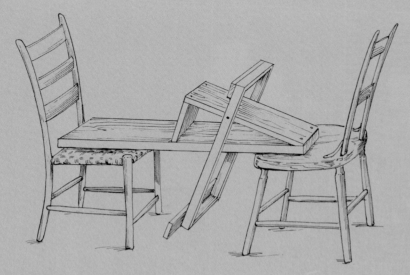

The shaving horse, like the chopping block, does not lend itself well to marketing, because one of its primary qualities is that this wonderfully simple, inexpensive tool can easily be made at home, by a novice, and will work the first time it's used.

light enough to carry over your shoulder, and with a new way of holding wood. I was delighted.

An elderly *seggellaio* had come to the priory to make chairs. He became ill and died there. His surname and village were unknown. When I visited a few years later, his equipment was just as he had left it. As noted above, Italians call this shaving horse *panko di seggellaio*. My French friends gave it the delightful name of *bicyclette de chaise* or "chair bicycle."

The attractiveness to children of this device for making shavings is very touching to see. Rarely have they had the opportunity to feel so safe and so powerful with a sharp tool. Both hands are needed to hold the drawknife, so fingers are kept out of the way of the cutting edge and—wonder of wonders—the wood stays firmly fixed. The harder you pull, the tighter the wood is gripped.

Friends were visiting from urban Minneapolis with their twelve-year-old daughter. She was bored, with no one her age around. Introduced to the shaving horse, and given a sharp drawknife and a piece of white cedar, she happily worked all day. After each break she headed back to the shop to make more of those beautiful curls.

I have not found shaving horses in use outside of Europe and direct cultural derivatives from there. If you have knowledge of other designs, other names, and other places where they can be found, please share them with me. I have a feeling that there are many delightful designs tucked away in the Balkans, the Caucasus, and the Pyrénées.

The accompanying drawing shows a shaving horse designed for making when time is of the essence and a number of horses are needed quickly. It can be made in an hour with hand tools. For simplicity's sake, legs are left off, as benches and chairs for support are usually plentiful.

I saw the mystic vision flow
And live in men and woods and streams
Until I could no longer know
The dreams of life from my own dreams

—A.E. (George Russell)

LIFE WORK

It is not enough to seek to design a society without war and violence. We need to eliminate the preconditions for violence as well. We need to design into society some of the positive factors that have drawn men into combat—the physical activity, the excitement, the *ésprit de corp*, and sense of urgency and camaraderie, a cause to identify with and to strive for, danger, risk, a feeling of importance and belonging.

The new pioneering will seek new ways to live, designing a society that will seek to fulfill each person's needs—a society that will encourage each person to develop to the fullest of their intellectual, physical, and creative potential. The world is greatly in need of such fully developed people and we have, at present, a society in which their presence is happenstance. It is bad psychology, bad sociology, bad economics, and just plain bad business.

We need a society that will not only banish warfare but also replace some of the roles war has played in people's lives—the excitement, the shared hardship, and the sense of common cause. Games such as football have been an attempt to provide such stimuli, but with the limitation of being competitive, and violent; another problem is that more people watch than play. Mountain climbing, whitewater canoeing, and skydiving are steps in the right direction, in that they are cooperative activities, exciting, close to nature, and do not seek to do violence. Yet these too are spare-time activities, peripheral to daily life.

A more positive example is taking a group of bored teenagers into the mountains to build a hut for emergency use, combining physical excitement with social service. Experience in the wilderness, combined with learning to use tools and building a shelter, makes a marvelous environment for growth.

Or mix the magic of gardening with both building and social action by getting a group of kids to work with the folks at the local retirement home to make a garden and construct a tool shed. You may find someone who is wise in horticulture but weak in the back who can be a guide for those who are short on knowledge but long on spading muscle. And building a homestead or a community on land that others considered to be useless can be an exciting challenge to all involved.

There have been many poets writing about nature, but mostly these have been people who were not close to nature in their daily lives. We need poets who can discover and proclaim the beauty of simplicity while themselves living a simple, rural life of creative and honest labor.

Rural Life

We are in need of a philosophy of rural living.

Civilization has tended to develop in urban centers. The magnets of companionship, money, markets, libraries, and so on have tended to draw great minds and talents to these centers. As a result we have developed philosophies based on an urban viewpoint, with rural, more decentralized communities no longer given respect. With the rapid increase in the ease of communication and

---

The one small garden of a free gardener was all his need and due, not a garden swollen to a realm; his own hands to use, not the hands of others to command.

—J.R.R. Tolkien

travel, many of the arguments in favor of urban living are invalidated. We are at an opportune time in history for the development of a culture that is decentralized, highly developed intellectually and physically, and active in bread labor.

There have been attempts in the past to develop such a rural culture, but the timing was not right. Gaining a livelihood took too much energy to have enough left over for creative thought. We have the potential to develop a rural culture that need apologize to none—exemplifying a life of intellect and labor, the blending of the best of mind and body in a creative harmony that will have intimate contact with nature and that will be refined in thought, in labor, in art and music and poetry.

We need a philosophy of rural living expressed in language that reflects rural associations and that gives meaning to daily life.

FAMILY LIFE

We need a way of life in which the whole family can play a visibly useful role, one where the very young and the very old can readily see that they are needed in the life of the family.

We cheat most children out of discovering the joy of learning to use their hands well—the productive work, creative activity, and mental growth that hand work can bring. We have managed to create a bland, emasculated world that gets its excitement from drugs, TV, spectator sports, and crime. So much adrenaline is being poured down a rat hole.

In our present society, one of the most exciting things a young person can do is to get involved in crime, either directly or vicariously through TV. A positive alternative is needed. Sports address some of these needs but only on a rather shallow level. They do not meet the challenge

Our keenest naturalists thrill to the falcon's breathtaking swoop or the leopard's sudden lunge from the dark. As for my excitement, I haven't found any need to travel to a tropical jungle. My Africa and Asia lie right outside my door—in grass where a yellow crab spider waits, two pairs of long arms tensed wide, eight eyes glittering.

—FRANK GRAHAM JR.

I often think today of what a difference it would make if children believed they were contributing to a family's survival and happiness. In the transformation from a rural to an urban society, children are robbed of the opportunity to do genuinely responsible work.

—DWIGHT D. EISENHOWER

When a man teaches his son no trade, it is as if he taught him highway robbery.

—THE TALMUD

of using one's energy and investing one's life in a productive way. Living close to wind and water, blizzard and frost; fishing for your food, as opposed to "sport" fishing; living close to the land; being responsible for one's own needs—all these can be productive and exciting. Boats have a special magic all their own. This special quality can be exploited in weekend regattas or can be used as a way to travel, to explore, to get food for a family. The designing and building of a craft to fit your own needs can become another potential challenge to the world of war, drugs, and crime.

What's needed are activities that draw the attention of the young and provide a dynamic alternative to the glitter of the town and the TV set. The axe and the canoe and the mountains are deep in the folklore of our culture. Most youngsters, given an introduction, find that these timeless sources of pleasure can hold their own with the excitement of motorcycles and the noise of rock and roll.

Once we have studied long and closely what makes a fine chair, then made and used our own, a chair will never look the same again. As we shape a thing with our mind and heart in the process, we come to an understanding of one more part of our world.

OPEN LETTER TO THOREAU

"The youth gets together his materials to build a bridge to the moon . . . and at length, the middle-aged man concludes to build a woodshed with them."

But Henry! We've done it, gone to the moon—and at such a price—while what we needed all along was a better woodshed.

We often hear the expression, "back to the land," or "back to the simple life," with the implication that life was better "back then." Was there ever a better time in which to live? At any rate, there is no turning back, so we'd best get on with the task of designing a better society.

The simple life that I'm advocating is a forward movement. "Down to earth" suits it better than "back to the land"—using our energies for solving problems of life here on earth rather than playing ring-around-the-moon with spaceships. We need to marshal all of our skills to move forward to a new way of life.

MEANING

We live in a world where the word "education" does not mean learning but merely schooling. "Civilization" does not mean cultivation and culture but rather nation-states spending astronomical amounts of wealth on preparation for war. "Food" does not mean nourishment but an endless array of substitutes, adulterants, preservatives, and growth hormones. "Shoe" does not mean footwear but foot ornament. And "freedom" does not mean liberty but wage slavery, welfare, and prostitution of labor.

If you were to buy a bottle to use as a bottle, and it leaked, you would have a legitimate complaint that you'd been sold a broken, unreliable, or inadequate bottle. And so it is with philosophy. The role of philosophy is to give

---

To be a philosopher is not merely to have subtle thoughts . . . but so to love wisdom as to live according to its dictates, a life of simplicity, independence, magnanimity and trust. It is to solve some of the problems of life, not only theoretically but practically.

—HENRY DAVID THOREAU

meaning and direction to daily life and only secondarily to provide intellectual exercise and an income to those who dwell in ivory towers. To the extent that a philosophy does not fulfill its primary purpose it is an incomplete, false, and leaky philosophy that should be returned to its maker with a complaint.

There is also a good deal of confusion about the word "technology," which is often used to mean something new and better. Technology, per se, is neither new nor better. It is as old as the digging stick, and has just as often been used to design weapons as beneficent inventions.

What we need now is a selective technology—tailored to fit our needs—a blend of the best of ancient and modern.

It is not only in the realm of technology that the minds of the ancients excelled. Some of the rules of conduct worked out thousands of years ago are still brilliantly applicable today. What more lovely gift have we had handed to us from the past than "Do unto others as you would have them do unto you . . ."?

> In these days of satellites and space stations, of UFOs
> and tales of visitors from other planets, I find
> I am not very interested in who might wander in
> from outer space. It is the little visitors
> from inner space—ideas!—that interest me.

RESPECTING OUR ELDERS?

One indication of the health of a society is its treatment of the elderly. A sensitive, thoughtful society will raise elderly people to positions of greater honor and respect as they grow older. This is not to argue in favor of a society tyrannized by the aged, but one in which seniors are cared for psychologically as well as physically, where their opinions are sought and valued. It is noble and

Among us English-speaking peoples especially do the praises of poverty need once more to be boldly sung. We have grown literally afraid to be poor. We despise anyone who elects to be poor in order to simplify and save his inner life. If he does not join the general scramble and pant with the money-making street, we deem him spiritless and lacking in ambition. . . . When we of the so-called better classes are scared as men never were scared in history at material ugliness and hardship; when we put off marriage until our house can be artistic, and quake at the thought of having a child without a bank-account and doomed to manual labor, it is time for thinking men to protest against so unmanly and irreligious a state of opinion. . . . I recommend this matter to your serious pondering, for it is certain that the prevalent fear of poverty among the educated classes is the worst moral disease from which our civilization suffers.

—WILLIAM JAMES

Scything

For my part, I'll take the scythe to cut the hay and the weeds. And why do I choose such an ancient tool when it has generally passed from the farm scene in America? Why have I resurrected this simple tool from the junk heap and restored its keen edge and gentle swing? The reasons are not many, but they are simple ones—like the tool itself:

First, the scythe is a quiet tool—one which allows its user to ponder sundry thoughts as he works in the dew of early morning (when the grass cuts best) and its sound disturbs no one, though right beneath a window.

Second, the scythe and the swinging thereof is, I find, a prime exercise and more in keeping with nature herself—"slow but sure"; and between the graceful swinging and advancing steps, time is taken to pause and sharpen the blade, allowing respites of rest.

Third, the perfume of the air roundabout is not disturbed with carbon monoxide.

Fourth, it is a light, mobile tool that can be taken between trees and boulders, down along a stream bed and up steep slopes.

Fifth, the cost is many times less than the machines which have replaced it, yet it will last longer and require less care.

Sixth, I find satisfaction in the history of this tool, its evolution, handed down and improved since biblical times, its grace, lightness and balance considered, and this or that changed—until we have a veritable Stradivarius of the fields.

—Daniel O'Hagan

beautiful to give respect to the elders as their physical powers wane, rather than to cast them aside. Neglect for the aged is not only ugly and lacking in gratefulness to the generation that cradled us and on whose shoulders we stand, it is myopic in the extreme, for we set an example in the treatment of our parents and grandparents that our children are likely to follow when we are old.

Searching for knowledge of simple living has brought me close to older people in a number of cultures. They have most willingly shared their knowledge. It is a crime that we do not design a way of living that fosters the use of our elders' minds and abilities.

A factor of inestimable psychological importance is feeling needed, and valuable. We benefit doubly by providing pleasant, useful work for older people: they benefit, through feeling needed; and society benefits from their contentedness and their contribution. Some of our most precious cultural treasures have come from minds well past three score years and ten. It is such a waste not to provide the optimal conditions for the maturing of wisdom.

In the society that I envision, there will be no problem of "retirement," the termination of work that was not fulfilling but was done out of economic necessity. When people are doing work they enjoy, retirement as we know it now will disappear. In its place will be the gradual lessening of work as energy wanes. To mind comes the picture of Scott Nearing in his late nineties, working each day in his garden, writing at the kitchen table, splitting wood, or collecting seaweed for compost. Contrast this with those who sit in their rooms, alone, watching the TV set and waiting for the end.

Borrow from cultures old and new
And with our imaginations
Blend those borrowings
To create new ways to live
That are simpler, gentler
More generous and beautiful

Cultural Blending

In searching for ideas from other cultures that can help us to build a better life, it is so enjoyable to discover something that has been handed down through the ages and is still useful today.

For instance, the working of green wood in the making of Windsor chairs is one of the most elegant, simple, and useful crafts ever invented. Such beautiful results from so little material. And the basic technique has changed little, if at all, since early times. Another example is woven cloth, which is primary to our lives in so many ways and as useful today as it was in biblical times. Likewise, the *umiak,* the large skin boat of the Alaskan Eskimos, was so highly refined in ages past that little, if any, improvement can now be made in its design.

Why all of this exuberance over finding that something old is good?

Maybe my pleasure is a result of the discovery that some aspects of life are so simple that they defy improvement. Perhaps I like the intimate feeling with the past that comes in realizing that some Asian shepherd, thousands of years ago, had the genius to make the first felt,

and the method was so wonderful, so efficient, and so easy that it continues basically unchanged to this day. Sitting here writing in my homemade felt boots gives me a feeling of kinship with that cultural ancestor. Such ties to the past may serve us as emotional sea anchors in the storms of rapid change that no doubt lie ahead.

Please understand that I am not suggesting that techniques and ideas are valid only because they are old. Both folk knowledge and folk ignorance have been handed down to us, and of course we need to distinguish between these. An example of the latter is the custom of painting a red band around the arm to prevent infection from spreading above that line.

Wisdom is too precious not to be gleaned wherever it can be found. Often new forms of wisdom can be discovered by comparing one culture or time with another. There is a special joy in finding that some ancient piece of knowledge can be tested and not found wanting.

I also get excited by those lovely hybrids that develop through cultural blending. An example of such blending is the crooked knife of the Tlingit Indians of the Northwest Coast (see page 114), which combines their traditional shape with modern steel and epoxy to create one

Curves: A Design Adventure

Since my first immersion in yurt design forty years ago, some kind of fascination with having more curved surfaces has been working in me.

This quest started with the roof, which seemed much more appealing with a curved profile.

For the Yurt Foundation letterhead, the logo that appealed to me most strongly had curvature in both the walls and the roof. But we all know that outward curving walls are impossible—aren't they?

Well—so I thought, these many years. Then—in the middle of the night—came a new design. Now, this is not my design, you understand. I had very little to do with it. There is a little humuncular fellow that advises me and lives somewhere upstairs, above my right ear. He is generous with his aid, if I give him free rein. His demands are twofold:

E. Miller

- go to bed at 9:00 P.M. sharp,
- do not take stimulants (meaning no coffee ice cream after noontime).

His design proposal was to use 3-inch-thick cedar for the walls and roof and put a curve in the wood (he neglected to show how).

My friend Tim, who lived in a forest surrounded by white cedar, had just purchased a new band-saw mill, with a horizontal blade. The challenge was to run cedar planks through the mill to get the proper curve.

Tim was willing and eager; this was the first project for the new mill. We thought of hanging the pieces of wood on a platform suspended overhead—a giant pendulum that could swing the plank through the saw. Here was an ingenious solution. We were ecstatic.

Then—we did some calculations and found the radius of the curve was some thirty feet … but we had no suspension point thirty feet high! And the inevitable elasticity in the suspension system would give an irregular cut.

There had to be another way. Another night, and—sure enough—that little fellow came to the rescue. We were to make a curved form twice the length of our plank and push the plank through the saw. We made up the form, locked the saw in place and shoved the first plank through. Hooray! It took only twenty seconds to cut the first piece.

The added magic of this method is that what appears at first to be waste wood is in fact the other side of the wall.

We built the one pictured here as our summer kitchen.

of the finest woodworking tools the world has known. These cultural hybrids are potentially infinite in number and variety, and they constitute one of the richest reservoirs of human endeavor.

Human Needs

For me it is ethically and economically indefensible not to use our efforts to meet human needs first. When someone is drowning, it would be the height of delusion to sit knitting a sweater, saying that the person will be cold upon coming from the water. What is needed is a rope now, and we'd best use all of our skill to find one with all possible speed.

The world is in dire need while we watch TV, play tennis, and do macramé.

To the suggestion that people also need pleasure and beauty—I agree wholeheartedly. But what I do not agree with is that pleasure and beauty reside exclusively in the realm of leisure and ornament. A rope, too, is a beautiful thing—especially when a life depends on it. Poverty and violence are ugly, and beauty can be found in opposing them as well as in sculpture, painting, and music.

I would like to see beauty all around us, not only in the things that are about us in our daily lives but also in how these things were made, in how we paid for them, in how our choices show that we treat our fellow dwellers on this earth with respect.

Take again my example of jogging: it does fine things for the body and the mind and can be a stimulus for creative thought, but the world is in an energy crisis and with all of the mental power represented by the joggers, we should be able to design activities that would provide all the benefits for mind and body that running provides, yet be able to store that energy for use. As a people, we have not accepted the fact that we live in a world in crisis.

The truth is that man needs work even more than he needs a wage. Those who seek the welfare of the workers, should be less anxious to obtain good pay, good holidays and good pensions for them than good work, which is the first of their goods. For the object of work is not so much to make objects as to make men. A man makes himself by making something useful.

—Mahatma Gandhi

Floss won't save you from an Abyss
But a rope will—
Not withstanding a Rope for a Souvenir
Is not beautiful—
But I tell you every step is a trough—
And every stop a Well—
Now will you have the Rope or the Floss
Prices reasonable—

—Emily Dickinson

Crooked Knives: Cultural Blending

There is a special magic in crooked knives. When I was a boy, if my father wanted to make a bowl or spoon, he needed a gouge, a mallet, a vise to hold the work, a bench to hold the vise, and a shop to hold the bench. With a crooked knife, all this gear is bypassed and you can sit by the fire and carve spoons and bowls.

Tim Smith was a kayak maker. We met in Alaska in the village of Hooper Bay. It was my first visit to an Eskimo village, and I was joyously blotting up new knowledge from all sides. Tim took me under his wing and answered all my queries about kayak making, *umiaks* (skin-covered boats), knife making, seal hunting, harpoon construction, and on and on. I wanted a Hooper Bay kayak in the worst way. He promised to either find one for me or sell me his.

We went seal hunting in his big *umiak* covered with split walrus hide. I was amazed to see it punch its way between cakes of ice. It would charge in, bounce back, and as the ice cakes moved apart the *umiak* passed between. With a wooden boat, this would have staved in the planks. When we sprang a leak in the *umiak*, someone merely stuffed a rag in the hole. This was the beginning of my love affair with skin boats.

W. Coperthwaite

W. Coperthwaite

D. Porter

We had all packed lunches. Mine was a sort of vegetable pemmican, a concentrated food called "grunch," easily carried, made of rolled oats, peanut butter, and honey. As I chewed on a lump sitting in this wonderful boat, my companions became curious.

"Would you like some?"

"Oh yes."

After the first round, I asked, "Would you like some more?"

"Oh yes."

Soon my rather ample supply had disappeared.

There is an Eskimo dish called *agutuk*, often referred to as Eskimo ice cream, made of whipped seal oil, berries, and sugar. *Agutuk* in Eskimo means something equivalent to "hash." My concoction was dubbed "*gussuk agutuk*" or "white man's hash". At odd times some of the crew would show up at my door and ask, "You got any more that *gussuk agutuk*?"

Back to Tim. He was a clever craftsman and a joy to be with. When he made a crooked knife, he did not forge it. He cold hammered it. First he found a butcher knife with steel that he liked, then shaped it with a file. Next with a sledgehammer head as an anvil he began peening the inside of the curve of the future crooked knife. While keeping pressure on the knife with one hand—as though springing in the curve—he would make many light blows with the ball of the hammer, striking directly above the contact point with the anvil. He slowly moved the blade about as the compressed steel started to curl up until 20 minutes later he had a crooked knife. To say I was fascinated would be an understatement. I was amazed. Here was democratic tool making at it's best.

During this period of my euphoria with everything Eskimo (well, almost everything), I assumed that his was an Eskimo invention. However, several years later I was in a village in Brittany with the wonderful name of Plougasneu (pronounced ploo-gaa-noo). A craftsman showed me the same technique for shaping steel, cold, with only a hammer and anvil. My suspicion is that this technique is very old and was known by the smiths on the early whaling ships in the Bering Sea.

The Eskimos were quick to see the value of this way of working steel and made it their own.

I bought Tim's kayak, and as I left the village he gave me his own crooked knife. For many years I used his kayak exploring the Maine coast. His knife is one of my finest, still getting daily usage.

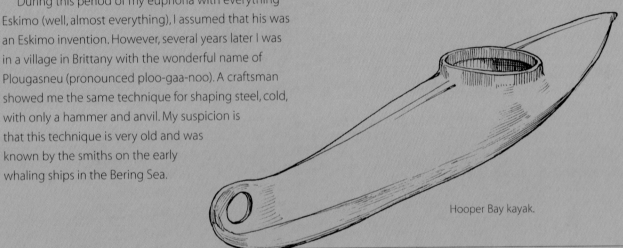

Hooper Bay kayak.

GRUNCH

The basic recipe consists of one handful of rolled oats, one heaping tablespoon of honey, and a heaping teaspoon of peanut butter. (If this sounds a bit off-putting, just imagine your favorite cake as a mess of flour, sugar, salt, and water, and see how appetizing that sounds.)

Mix the honey and peanut butter thoroughly in a bowl by mashing the mixture with a spoon, then mix in the oats. When fully mixed the grunch will stick together but not to your hands. That's it.

*The real voyage of discovery lies not in seeking new places
but in seeing with new eyes.*

—Marcel Proust

I, too, like to run and have spent many years doing so, but I am now seeking a more satisfying outlet for this energy, a release that feels good to my conscience as well as my body. Chopping wood, for instance. It is productive and satisfying and offers good mental time as well.

Recently, I've rediscovered the sledgehammer. There are ledges in the middle of the beach here that interfere with landing the canoes. These respond—with some reluctance—to some nudging with a 16-pound maul. Beating on the ledges gives my heart and lungs all of the activity they want, plus the best rock music I've heard.

You respond that you haven't any ledges, and nary a beach either? How about grinding your own grain in a hand mill or quern? It is good exercise, and the freshly ground flour gives added nutrition and flavor to homemade bread and cereals. On top of this comes the good feeling of doing something pleasant and productive without wasted energy. Driving fence posts, removing stumps, building rock walls—there are myriad ways in which the same effect can be achieved, if we put our minds to the challenge. Try mowing your lawn or cutting hay for a cow or goat with a good scythe—it will eliminate the noise and fumes of the power mower and give exercise and satisfaction as well.

I want to live in a society where people
are intoxicated with the joy of making things.

Pioneering

Pioneers are needed today more than at any time in the past, not for exploring the ocean depths, the tops of mountains, nor the vast unknowns of space, but for finding new ways to build a better world.

We need pioneers to design a gentle society such as has never been seen before, where all people will have the freedom to develop to their limits. This is the greatest challenge we have, making the climbing of Everest seem to be a Sunday afternoon stroll by comparison.

The enlightened prospecting of the future will not be for mineral wealth, and the treasure found will not be gold and rubies. Riches of a far rarer sort will be sought—the knowledge of how to create a society in which everyone is decently clothed, fed, and sheltered, with the opportunity to grow to be fully mature, creative people. We must discover how to have a happier, healthier family and community life.

We have the knowledge and the resources to accomplish all of this. The parts of the puzzle are all present, yet finding how to put them together is the great challenge.

Life can be viewed as a huge treasure hunt where all are seeking what they deem to be of value. To the extent that the things we seek are limited in supply (money, fame, victory) there will be strife. But to the extent that we seek treasures that deprive no one (wisdom, health, skill) or treasures that help others (love, friendship, justice) we take part in building a better world.

We can view the search for a better world
as exploration. We may discover that the expedition
is the better world and that our own most important
discoveries will be along the lines of how to improve
the expedition—how to get others to join
and help in the search.

I, for one, do not have answers to the problem of how to build a better world, here and now—how to build such a world without harming others and without excessive use of the world's resources. Finding those answers is the ultimate challenge, and this is the pioneering that needs to be done.

The search for ways to create this better world is one of the most exciting, challenging, and physically and intellectually demanding quests ever undertaken. It is invigorating to be living in a time when humanity has developed to the point where we actually have the basic knowledge needed for solving our problems. Working toward this goal is the most exciting game in town—and the most worth playing.

People casually say, "There is nothing new under the sun." Poppycock. Doing something new is not hard (putting wheels on a bird house, for example). Doing something that is both new and useful, that is more difficult. But, doing something that is new, useful, and *better*—that is rare indeed, and therein lies the challenge.

If we could encourage people everywhere to get involved in this search, we would have an unprecedented collection of talent engaged in the work. We would have many ideas for new solutions—and better ones, and less rarely. One measure of a healthy, mature, and creative society will be that people will value their own development and follow where this leads. As Thoreau wrote, "Do what you love. Know your own bone. Gnaw it. Bury it. Unearth it and gnaw it still."

This is the true joy of life, the being used up for a purpose recognized by yourself as a mighty one; being a force of nature instead of a feverish, selfish little clod of ailments and grievances, complaining that the world will not devote itself to making you happy.

I am of the opinion that my life belongs to the community, and as long as I live, it is my privilege to do for it whatever I can. I want to be thoroughly used up when I die, for the harder I work, the more I live.

Life is no "brief candle" to me. It is a sort of splendid torch which I have got hold of for a moment, and I want to make it burn as brightly as possible before handing it on to future generations.

—George Bernard Shaw

First paperback printing March, 2007.

16 17 18 19   8 7 6 5

Portions of the text, sometimes in different versions, have been previously published in *Manas* and *Mother Earth News*.
The author expresses gratitude to the editors of these journals.

Library of Congress Cataloging-in-Publication Data
Coperthwaite, William S.
 A handmade life / William S. Coperthwaite.
  p. cm.
 ISBN 1-931498-25-3 (alk. paper) **(hardcover)**
 1. Social sciences—Philosophy. 2. Humanism. I. Title.

H61.15.C66 2003
300'.1—dc21
                                        2003046208

ISBN: 978-1-933392-47-9 **(pbk.)**

Chelsea Green Publishing
85 North Main Street, Suite 120
White River Junction, VT 05001
(802) 295-6300
www.chelseagreen.com

FSC
www.fsc.org
MIX
Paper from
responsible sources
FSC® C101537

With deep admiration this book is dedicated to

WALTER CLARK

1905–1981

The finest educator it is my privilege
to have known.

MY THANKS TO ALL who have helped in this effort. To the folks at Chelsea Green who have guided me through the process of creating a book. Special thanks go to Jim Schley, my editor, and to Ann Aspell, the designer.

It is by the patient encouragement of John Saltmarsh and Peter Forbes that this book sees the light of day.

Many eyes and hands have helped with this manuscript: Jo Anna Allen, Sonni Chamberland, Nancy Ellinwood, Greg Farrell, Henry Geiger, Tom and Julie Henze, Mary Hinerman, Becky Kemery, Annette Lasley, Claire Holland LeClair, Brenda Lehman, Dan Neumeyer, and Helen Whybrow.

I welcome letters at Wm. Coperthwaite, Dickinsons Reach, Machiasport, Maine 04655.

Excerpts from the work of Emily Dickinson are reprinted by permission of the publishers and the Trustees of Amherst College from *The Poems of Emily Dickinson,* edited by Thomas H. Johnson, Cambridge, Mass.: The Belknap Press of Harvard University Press, copyright 1951, 1955, 1979 by the President and Fellows of Harvard College.

"What is He?" by D.H. Lawrence is reprinted with permission from *The Complete Poems of D.H. Lawrence* by D.H. Lawrence, edited by V. de Sola Pinto and F. W. Roberts, copyright 1964, 1971 by Angelo Ravagli and C.M. Weekly, executors of the estate of Frieda Lawrence Ravagli. Used by permission of Viking Penguin, a division of Penguin Putnam, Inc.

ABOUT THE AUTHOR

WILLIAM COPERTHWAITE was a native of Maine who traveled the world in search of folk-art techniques and subsistence skills. Impressed by the beauty and intelligence of the traditional central Asian nomadic tents called "yurts," Coperthwaite adapted and introduced to North America yurt design and construction. For four decades he participated in building more than three hundred yurts for family homes, schools, camps, and outbuildings. Awarded a doctorate from Harvard University's School of Education for his work with Eskimo villagers, Coperthwaite taught in a variety of innovative educational settings. William passed away unexpectedly in late 2013. His organization, the Yurt Foundation, continues to serve to promote sensible and economical self-reliance through workshops, lectures, and publications.

Peter Forbes is a writer, photographer, and long-time leader in the American land conservation movement. You can learn more about him at Peterforbes.org.

the politics and practice of sustainable living

CHELSEA GREEN PUBLISHING

Chelsea Green Publishing sees books as tools for effecting cultural change and seeks to empower citizens to participate in reclaiming our global commons and become its impassioned stewards. If you enjoyed *A Handmade Life*, please consider these other great books related to biography and memoir.

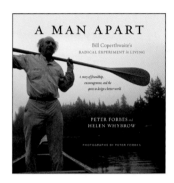

A MAN APART
Bill Coperthwaite's Radical Experiment in Living
PETER FORBES and HELEN WHYBROW
9781603585477
Hardcover • $35.00

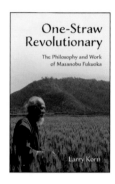

ONE-STRAW REVOLUTIONARY
The Philosophy and Work of Masanobu Fukuoka
LARRY KORN
9781603585309
Paperback • $19.95

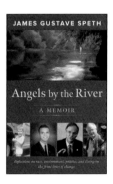

ANGELS BY THE RIVER
A Memoir
JAMES GUSTAVE SPETH
9781603586320
Paperback • $17.95

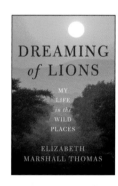

DREAMING OF LIONS
My Life in the Wild Places
ELIZABETH MARSHALL THOMAS
9781603586399
Paperback • $17.95

CHELSEA GREEN PUBLISHING
the politics and practice of sustainable living

For more information or to request a catalog,
visit **www.chelseagreen.com** or
call toll-free **(800) 639-4099**.